THE CLIMB
6 STEPS TO A POWERFUL PERSONAL BRAND

D.K. SUTTON

Copyright © 2019 by Dwayne K. Sutton

All rights reserved. No part of this publication may be reproduced, distributed, or transmitted in any form or by any means, including photocopying, recording, or other electronic or mechanical methods, without the prior written permission of the publisher, except in the case of brief quotations embodied in critical reviews and certain other noncommercial uses permitted by copyright law. For permission requests, send a message to the publisher, addressed "Attention: Permissions Coordinator," at the web address below.

Parrish Street Press
Huntersville, North Carolina
www.parrishstreetpress.com

Ordering Information:
Quantity sales: Special discounts are available on quantity purchases by corporations, associations, and others. For details, contact the publisher at the address above.

ISBN: 9781079731309

Printed in the United States of America

This book is dedicated to those entrepreneurs, game-changers, and transformational leaders who dare to make meaning with their work.

Table of Contents

THE CLIMB.. i
INTRODUCTION 1
   THE CLIMB 3
WHAT IS A BRAND? 23
   CHAPTER 1 23
      THE BILLION DOLLAR QUESTION: WHAT IS A BRAND?23
STEP 1: BRAND VALUES.. 31
   CHAPTER 2 33
      THE MAGNETIC FORCE 33
   CHAPTER 3 41
      YOUR PERSONAL VALUES 41
      PERSONAL VALUES WORKSHEET 45
   CHAPTER 4 49
      YOUR VALUES IN ACTION 49
STEP 2: YOUR BRAND STORY 55
   CHAPTER 5 57
      YOUR BRAND STORY 57
   CHAPTER 6 61
      ANATOMY OF A COMPELLING STORY 73
   CHAPTER 7 79
      STORY EXAMPLES 79
   CHAPTER 8 83
      DISCOVERING YOUR STORY 83
   STORY SYNOPSIS... 61
   THE SHAWSHANK REDEMPTION SYNOPSIS 63
   SNOW WHITE STORY SYNOPSIS........................ 67
   TOMS SHOES ORIGIN STORY 71
STEP 3: BRAND POSITIONING............................ 89
   CHAPTER 9 91

BRAND POSITIONING INTRODUCTION 91
CHAPTER 10 101
FINDING YOUR POSITION IN THE MARKET 101
CHAPTER 11 107
EXAMPLES OF POSITIONING 107
STEP 4: BRAND PERSONALITY 109
CHAPTER 12 111
BRAND PERSONALITY INTRODUCTION 111
CHAPTER 13 115
DISCOVERING YOUR BRAND PERSONALITY 115
STEP 5: BRAND IDENTITY 119
CHAPTER 14 121
BRAND IDENTITY 121
CHAPTER 15 125
THE BRAND IDENTITY PROCESS 125
STEP 6: BRAND YOU 135
CHAPTER 16 137
ACTION STEPS 137
ABOUT THE AUTHOR 143

INTRODUCTION

THE CLIMB

Several years ago, I was sitting and chatting backstage with a recording artist after one of his shows. We had a typical conversation - one I've had with him and others many times before. We told stupid jokes, and laughed at how stupid the jokes were, took jabs at each other about our favorite sports teams, and even managed to sprinkle in a little politics.

It had been a few months since I had seen him, so jabbing, laughing and, yeah, debating was warranted.

Then, suddenly, the room became eerily silent. He took in a deep breath through his nostrils, slightly lowered his head, wiped post performance sweat from a brow, and exhaled rapidly through his opened mouth.

With his head rising he said, "You know man, I want to be like you. Yeah. You are free and I'm not."

Confused, I just sat and looked at him like a parent waiting for bad news. But I knew that there was more. So, I waited.

Then he went on.

"See, I just performed in front of 18,000 people. Tomorrow, I will perform in front of 20,000 people, just in a different town. Still, tomorrow morning, I'm going to wake up broke."

THE CLIMB

Whoa. His revelation hit me in the middle of my chest like the force of a 230-pound running back.

This time, though, I didn't have the luxury of waiting. Whether I liked it or not, it was my turn to speak.

I took a few seconds, although it felt like a few minutes, to collect my thoughts. I looked at him, smiled, and responded with, "Then we're going to have to help you wake up wealthy."

He smiled. I smiled. We smiled.

And just like that, a new journey began for him and for me.

Although I had given him high-level business advice throughout his relatively short career, I was not familiar with the daily intricacies of his professional and personal life. I didn't know, for example, if he owned businesses, real estate or his master recordings. Sure, I had heard the rumors about his precarious financial situation. Huh, that's pretty much the story for every recording artist, right? Still, the whispers about him "not doing well" were just rumors and I learned a long time ago that rumors are a dangerous place to start a conversation.

Despite our loose history, I felt compelled to help him at a deeper level than I had in the past. I love to see people win. I especially love seeing people who are younger than me win.

I have always been a big believer in maximizing the opportunity that's right in front of me. And, well, he was sitting right in front of me. So, why not begin the process of transformation in his dressing room.

Introduction

THE JOURNEY BEGINS

To start, I did what any good mentor or adviser would do. I asked a lot of questions.

I began with simple questions; you know, yes and no type questions. Then I moved into open-ended questions; the questions where you must think about your answers.

Within a few minutes, and a few questions, it became crystal clear to me what the real issue was as it related to his career in general and his finances, specifically.

See, at the time, he was a rising star with two hits on the charts. To support those songs, he made a few appearances on awards shows, performed his hit songs on national morning and late-night television programs, and toured. You know, he did the typical stuff.

Still, he wasn't a big star with a big name making big money. Well, truth be told, even if he was, he would have been facing the same issues.

The problem was, like most musicians, he made most of his money from touring and spot performances. Typical. Nothing to see here. Ah, but he controlled no aspect of his music finances. None. That was issue number one. After management and a host of other mysterious fees, he was left with enough money to pay his already modest bills.

Okay, but, what about his big spending?

Well, unlike many recording artists, he was not flashy or a big spender. He didn't have a leased Bentley, wear a diamond-studded necklace, or own custom clothing. Actually, he was as plain as they

THE CLIMB

come. He rented a small home and paid for its upkeep through tour dollars while he was on the road.

You see, his problem wasn't spending. His problem was limited income. To be succinct, he only had one significant source of income and that was money from touring. And, as I mentioned before, he controlled practically none of what came in and what went out.

Okay, so, the plan was simple: create assets that he controlled. The first asset we focused on was his person; his brand.

Brands, whether tangible or intangible, like a personal brand, are assets. At the time, for all intents and purposes, he wasn't a brand.

Now, you're probably wondering, "Why focus on building his brand?"

When you study the value of companies we love, you will find that much of their value comes from their brand - an intangible asset. Coca-Cola is a prime example. Its brand is valued at $73.1 billion (2018).

In the case of this recording artist, I knew that his personal brand and the income streams that would come from it would be his biggest asset. We only need to think of Jordan Brand or Kylie Jenner, the youngest "self-made" billionaire, to understand the impact of a personal brand. As I will discuss in detail later, personal brands enjoy benefits and advantages non-brands don't. One big one is income.

Introduction

Simply put, powerful personal brands can command salaries, prices and fees that are easily 10, 100, or 1,000 times more than non-brands.

Again, I'll go into greater detail later.

POPULAR OR A BRAND?

First, before we go deeper, a quick word about branding. Just because you're popular, or somewhat well-known, it doesn't mean that you are a brand. They are two completely different animals. Remember, there have been lots of one hit wonders - here today, gone tomorrow.

To that end, the first rule of branding is you must have a good product or service. You can't build a powerful brand on the back of a broken product. Many have tried and all have failed.

Fortunately for him, though, he did have a good product, if you will - meaning his talent. No, you don't have to be the best - whatever that is. But you can't be the worst.

Again, he was a good product. He was genuinely talented, although that's not necessary these days, and he was a good person. Still, he wasn't a brand; he didn't have a story. Let me explain.

THE STORY

Okay, everything about you tells a story. Yes, everything. Your style of dress, personality, logo, signature, colors, bumper stickers, building location, slogan, employees, presentation style, website, product packaging, about page, Instagram posts, and Tweets, just to name a few, say who you are and who you are not in a matter of

THE CLIMB

moments. The problem is, like him, most don't have a clue what story they're telling. And that's not good.

See, when you don't know your story, every time a fan, customer, client, or patient comes into contact with you, they leave with a different message. Because they leave with a different message, each contact with you leaves them confused about who you are and how you can make their lives better. As such, incredible business and financial opportunities are left on the table. Get it?

FIND THE STORY AND WIN
Yeah, not knowing his story was his biggest problem. I saw it as my responsibility to help him fix that issue.

Through the brand auditing process, I discovered his strengths, for which there were many, and his weaknesses. More importantly, we discovered his story. I will walk you through the process, step-by-step, later in the book.

Today, he is a recognized brand with 11 streams of income. He no longer relies on his music income to live. Yup, things have worked out quite well for him and, yes, me.

HOW I GOT HERE
The more success he found the more word began to spread. Within a relatively short period of time, I found myself becoming the go-to person for literally hundreds of entertainers seeking to build their brand, grow their following and skyrocket their income. Soon, celebrity chefs, real estate professionals, professional athletes, health and legal experts, consultants, and public speakers came calling.

Introduction

With each new engagement, I realized that I needed a system. I needed a method for on-boarding new clients quickly and effectively. I needed a system that would ensure that they made it the top of their market and top of mind. Thus, the name, The Climb.

There was no blueprint. It was trial and error. Okay, it was more error than trial. Fortunately, the results were incredible.

Over time, I enhanced The Climb system. In some cases, I took elements out. In other cases, I added thought pieces, readings, and exercises in.

Through many iterations, The Climb system has been incredibly successful. Chefs have their own cooking channels, unknown authors have published bestsellers, physicians appear regularly in the media as medical experts, entertainers endorse major products and photographers, among hundreds of others, now command top fees for their work.

The Climb system works and I'm proud of this fact.

SHARING THE KNOWLEDGE

Unfortunately, my work was only available to those professionals who could afford my high coaching fees. I wanted to change this fact but didn't know how without diluting my own brand. That's when client and Grammy and Song of the Year (Ed Sheeran's "The Shape of You") winning entertainment executive Tony Mercedes suggested that I make my work available to a wider audience through some type of course format. I took his advice and launched several online courses on branding.

THE CLIMB

Frankly, it was simply an experiment. I didn't expect much. I honestly didn't believe that my style of coaching and advising would translate effectively to an online course. I was wrong.

During the first 18 months, over 29,400 people from 141 countries paid to learn personal branding from me. I honestly didn't expect this success and certainty not that fast. The truth is, being an international bestseller is awesome. However, seeing thousands transform their businesses and careers is even sweeter.

Here's the thing: I wrote this book to help you build a world class brand and eventually realize unprecedented financial success.

TO BRAND OR NOT TO BRAND

Now, you may be wondering, "Is it even necessary to build a brand? Besides, I'm not popular or well known. Will it really make a difference to my long-term success? Is the effort worth my time and money?"

Let's address these questions.

As I stated before, powerful brands enjoy advantages non-brands don't. They command higher fees and salaries, get referred more often, are quoted in the media, enjoy a high level of trust, win endorsements, are thought of first, and they have the benefit of market momentum.

Let's look at these advantages one-by-one.

1. Personal Brands Command Higher Fees and Salaries

Take personal financial guru Suze Orman. You may know her name from her time on the Oprah Winfrey show, through her bestselling books, or her public broadcasting specials. Her brand has allowed her to command high six-figure book advances while others are fortunate to receive a few thousand dollars. Okay, true, she is now well-known. Ah, but it wasn't always that way. Still, admittedly, her brand, like it does for all powerful personal brands, gives her market momentum.

What about Dr. Sampson Davis? Wait, you've never heard of him? Well, the right people have. He receives $25,000 or more in speaking fees for a 90-minute talk. Other active speakers are lucky to get $2,500 per talk.

An artist with an established brand is offered hundreds and thousands of times more for his paintings or photography. Other artists? Huh, you've heard the one about starving artists, right? Yeah, it's real.

But then there's photographer Peter Lik. He sells his landscape photos for tens of thousands of dollars apiece. Many go for well over $100,000 each. Former U.S. president Bill Clinton and rock star Bono, among many others, have by spent over $100,000 for Lik's work. By the way, Lik recently sold a photograph for $6 million dollars. Let that sink in for a moment.

In music, the numbers are staggering. Personal brands like Lady Gaga, Beyonce, Kanye West, and the Rolling Stones are offered $300,000 or more per show while most musicians are overjoyed making $500 a week.

Several times a year, thousands of people eagerly pay thousands of dollars to attend a Tony Robbins seminar. He commands as much as $1 million from just one coaching client.

THE CLIMB

Speaking of coaching, personal brands command hundreds and sometimes thousands of dollars per hour for their coaching. I'm by no means famous. Huh, not even close. Yet, you can't book me for a coaching session for less than $10,000 for a single day. Obviously, there are few who can afford such high fees. But, for them the return far exceeds the fee. Still, this is the power of a brand. Again, being popular doesn't mean that you're a brand.

2. Personal Brands Receive A Flood of Referrals

Referrals are critical to growing your business, practice, or fan base. First, it is a form of the most powerful marketing tool ever - word of mouth. In other words, it's free, in most cases, and powerful.

When you are referred by another, it means that person is putting her reputation on the line. That's a major gesture for someone you may know and even more so for a stranger. She, the person making the referral, is essentially saying, "I give you my word that this is the right person to help solve your problem."

Such a referral has the force of 100 content pieces on your blog. It establishes your credibility and vouches for your expertise.

In the end, a referral can mean that you won't have to haggle as much over price, if at all.

Finally, being referred also reduces your marketing costs. Why? Again, most referrals are free.

3. Personal brands are frequently quoted in the media.

Have you ever noticed that certain fitness, health, medical, or legal experts show up on television, online, or in print on a regular basis? Well, I can assure you, it is not by accident.

By being frequently quoted in the media, their credibility is enhanced. The world thinks, "They must be good, right? Besides, they are always quoted in the media."

Well, maybe.

Whether we believe that they are good or not is irrelevant. Their audience members believe that they are good, and this media exposure further cements this belief. Besides, it's difficult to take life-altering advice from someone you've never heard of.

4. Personal Brands Enjoy A High Level of Trust

Being a physician, for example, comes with its own level of credibility and trust. But when you are a physician and a brand, the level of trust for you goes through the roof.

Dr. Oz, for example, can change an entire industry by pointing out health concerns with a food product. This happened when he pointed out the levels of arsenic in apple juice. Some of his colleagues disagreed with him. However, the public sided with Oz. That's the power of a brand.

5. Personal Brands Win Endorsements

Smooth Jazz musician Mike Phillips has built an incredible following for a relatively unknown musician. He has hundreds of thousands of followers and his fans look forward to him coming to their town.

THE CLIMB

Phillips has brilliantly turned his following into coveted endorsement deals. He, for example, is the first non-athlete to win an endorsement deal with Nike, or more specifically, the Jordan brand. Unheard of.

*In the interest of full disclosure, I've had the pleasure of working directly with Mike for many years and he is a dear friend. I was his personal manager and advise him to this day.

6. Personal Brands Have the Benefit of Momentum.

Here's what I mean: Fitness guru Mike Chang has amassed a huge online following. His YouTube videos have been viewed over four billion (4,000,000,000) times. Yep, that's four billion. He also has over four million YouTube subscribers.

See, once Chang got the first million views, which is not easy to do, momentum kicked in. But, let's back up for a moment.

The achievement of a "million" anything gives legitimacy to an endeavor. For example, how is success measured in the record industry? In millions, right? They even have a term for it: going platinum.

Is it any wonder, then, that practically all television talent shows offer one million dollars as a prize?

The thing is, once you hit a million, it gives those sitting on the fence an incentive to hop off. It also attracts those who would have otherwise been disinterested.

Momentum. It's a great thing.

So, there you have them. Let's recap. Personal brands command higher fees, get referred more often, is frequently quoted in the media, enjoy a high level of trust, win endorsements, and enjoy market momentum.

Is Branding by Accident or by Design?

Okay, here's the big question: how did they get there? How did they get to enjoy such a privileged position? What is their magic?

First, let's deal with another question: Is their success by accident or by design?

Huh, great question, right?

Yes, there are those who fall into notoriety. We see it all the time. Someone posts a YouTube video and it goes viral. They are interviewed on television and radio. They gain some traction. They may even hang around for two days. But can that popularity carry? In most cases, it can't.

Now, I can just hear the screams. What about the Kardashians? True. They are famous for, huh, being famous.

But the Kardashians' fame started with Kim's infamous sex tape. Of course, she wasn't the only one to be involved in a normally career-ending scandal. Granted, she didn't have a career prior to the sex tape.

For example, actor Rob Lowe's career was sidelined after his, uh, exposure. He has, after many years, rebounded.

Now, what Kim Kardashian had that others didn't was her mother Kris. By all accounts, she's a marketing and branding mastermind.

THE CLIMB

Instead of seeing the sex tape as a setback, Kris saw it as a setup for something much bigger - the Kardashian brand.

Today, Kim alone makes tens of millions of dollars a year from her cadre of apps, makeup, clothing, and other entrepreneurial ventures. Yes, she is popular. But she is now a brand, thanks to mommy.

Branding is by Design

See, branding is a strategic and well-thought-out move. You don't pick your brand colors by accident. You don't develop a core brand message by accident. You don't infuse your brand personality in television ads, Tweets, FaceBook posts and Blogs by accident. You don't learn and live your core brand values by accident.

It is all by design. Kris Jenner understood this fact and so do powerful personal brands.

Okay, so how did these personal brands become powerful personal brands?

Remember, everything about them tells a story. Their website, blog, about page, colors, logo, product names, book titles, seminars, speeches, and interviews. Yes, everything.

The difference is they know and tell a compelling, consistent and congruent story. This story makes a connection with their audience, or what I like to call their tribe. It is this story that changes the game.

Introduction

See they began with things like their personal values. They are not afraid to say what they stand for. They are not afraid to show what's important to them.

Financial guru Dave Ramsey stands for peace. Specifically, peace that comes from being debt free. In fact, his bestselling course is entitled Financial Peace University. Through his course and media interviews, he's willing to challenge anyone and any organization about the perils of debt. He is unwavering in this belief.

Lady Gaga is about openness, tolerance, and creative expression. These values are demonstrated in her songs, concerts, and interviews. There are millions of people who resonate with those values. She calls them Little Monsters (her tribe).

My job, in this book, is to help you discover and tell your story and help you make the climb to the top of your field.

What to Expect from this Book

In this book, we will walk, step-by-step through the process of telling your story. Like with the powerful personal brands we have discussed, we will discover your driving values, position you in the minds of your audience members, and create your identity pieces like your logo, among other activities.

Now, let me say this: this book is based on actual, in the field, practical work. I'm talking direct work with real people. I'm speaking of my work with Grammy and Emmy Award winners, medical correspondents, professional athletes, television personalities, celebrity personal trainers, international recording artists, elected officials, and many others.

THE CLIMB

Okay, so what can you expect after you read this book? Will you become a powerful personal brand?

Nope. I doubt it.

That's because building a brand takes time. Yes, there are some activities that will establish your expertise and make you a media source in a matter of weeks. I will share with you exactly how to do that.

Still, it all depends upon your effort.

Sure, I recently helped an unknown musician land 17 interviews with local and national magazines in a three-week period. He sold more records and booked more shows during that time period than he had in his entire 12-year career.

And, yes, I helped a physician become a highly sought-after media source and recognized expert in just six weeks.

Again, I don't know if you will see similar results. It depends upon how good you are at what you do and the effort you put into working the program.

Here's what I know for sure: the program works. There is just no question about it.

So, here's my promise to you: If you read the book, and follow through, you will learn:

- What qualities automatically attract the right audience to you. Once you discover who you really are as a personal brand, you will attract raving fans or committed clients.

Introduction

- Why people like Lady Gaga, Tony Robbins and many others are so beloved and how you can tap into this same energy.
- How to easily make the right decisions, enter the right relationships and set the right goals when building your personal brand.
- How to introduce yourself to your target, your tribe, in such a way that they immediately feel a genuine connection with you. It's a lot simpler than you think. The cool part is, you can just be yourself and win.
- How to write an about page that captures and holds the attention of all of those who visits your website. They will find it difficult to turn away.
- How to tell a compelling brand story in 45 seconds that has the same appeal as a two-hour blockbuster movie.
- The five elements that make up a compelling story and how to apply this template to your personal brand. Hollywood has been using this template for years to suck you in. You will learn how to apply this same template, although my version, into your life and career.
- How to stand out from your competition no matter how crowded your market or how well funded they are.
- Why you always think of a specific brand when you think of a certain situation. More importantly, you will learn how to get others to think of you when they think of a certain situation.
- Learn how to answer with power and authority when someone asks, "What do you do?" You will learn how to be unforgettable even when your time is short.
- How to make radio, television audiences fall in love with you when you talk about yourself.
- How to choose the right colors, logo and packaging for your brand. Yep, as a personal brand, you especially need this stuff.

THE CLIMB

- And much, much more.

Finally, I take a practical approach in my work. I don't believe in fluff. I believe in, and teach, from my personal experience and those I've helped.

The point is, this is real stuff - actual actionable steps.

Enough said. It's time for you to start making the climb to the top.

Right now.

WHAT IS A BRAND?

CHAPTER 1

THE BILLION DOLLAR QUESTION: WHAT IS A BRAND?

Each year, organizations like Brand Finance, a brand consultancy, issues their ranking of the world's most valuable brands. By looking at factors such as stakeholder investment, business performance, and marketing costs, they assess how each brand contributes to the overall value of the company. In 2018, Amazon finally surpassed Google as the most valuable brand. Apple, which has been in the second-place spot for the past several years, remained in that spot.

Whether we are speaking of FaceBook, AT&T or Microsoft, they all have one thing in common: a recognizable brand. In fact, it is believed that Coca-Cola's brand is more valuable than all its physical assets combined. In an age where many brands manufacture little this is not a surprise.

Okay, fine. But what is a brand? Is it a logo? Or, is it the colors or a slogan? I mean, what in the world is a brand?

Ah, that's the billion-dollar question, right?

Well, to many, a brand is simply a logo. That's what they see. But, is a brand simply a logo? Is that it?

To answer that question, I'm going to ask you one: What type car is BMW?

THE CLIMB

Most people would say that BMW is a luxury car. Their cars are premium-priced, have high-end features and are compared to autos in the luxury category. So, this determination makes sense.

Let's explore this premise of BMW being a luxury car by reviewing their marketing. Because if BMW considers themselves a luxury car manufacturer, they would certainly say so.

We will start by going to their website and snooping around. Next, let's review their marketing. If there's ever a place to get to this luxury answer, their marketing is it.

First, we're hit up YouTube and study their ads. Then we're do a Google search for their cause-marketing campaigns. Yeah, that should do it.

After an exhaustive search, we realize that we can't find the word luxury anywhere. We can't find it on their website or in their television, print or online ads.

Huh? Wait, what?

Yeah, it turns out that BMW doesn't use the word luxury in the marketing of their cars. This means that they don't consider their cars luxury cars.

Why do you think that is?

See, the promise that BMW makes is, "If you buy our cars, you're going to have the best driving experience of your life."

What is a brand?

To be more succinct, their brand is about the driving experience - yup, the driving experience. Remember, they don't make cars. They make ultimate driving machines. Get it?

This means that their logo is just one part of their brand. Their logo, then, is simply a means of identifying their cars, I mean, ultimate driving machines.

BMW makes beautiful cars. But they make cars that drive exceptionally well. This is their difference.

This concept of the ultimate driving experience is so important to BMW that they include it in all their marketing and philanthropic work. For example, when they supported Susan G. Komen's Race for the Cure, they called their participation, "The Drive for the Cure".

It's about the drive, not the logo.

THE LOGO. IT'S PART OF A BIGGER PICTURE.
We just established that a logo is simply one part of a brand. Okay, that means that there are other elements that make up a brand besides a logo, right? So, what are those other elements?

The best way to understand a brand, and brand elements, is by taking a trip to the grocery store. Come along with me.

Okay, we hop in our car and head to a local supermarket for, say, red apples. We drive for a few minutes and eventually arrive and park. We exit our car, walk towards the store and enter the automatic doors. Having been at this store before, we know where the apples are and immediately make a b-line to the produce section.

THE CLIMB

As usual, we see a variety of fruits and vegetables as we pass a forest of colors. There are literally thousands of items. Some are labeled as organic and others of, well, questionable origin. But we are only are interested in apples. Specifically, we want red ones. So, we trek to that section.

We get to the apple section and see a cornucopia of colors. There are green, yellow, mixed and, of course, red apples. We're not apple experts. So, we walk towards the closest thing to a red apple we can find. Ah, yes. There they are.

We pick up one and rub our thumb across it. We look closely at it. Then we look at another and another. Huh, they all look and feel the same. In fact, if we went to another grocery chain store, we could find similar red apples. Huh, they might even be from the same grower. Interesting.

Ah, right. And that's when we learn our first branding lesson: we literally have no way of knowing if there really is any difference between the apples we are holding and those at another store - even those that are from the same chain store. Because they are not differentiated, we can't tell them apart from any other red apple. As such, these apples are commodities. And that's a really big problem, from a branding standpoint.

See, when something is a commodity, price becomes really important. Again, because the apples aren't differentiated, we, the consumer, don't see them as being any different from another red apple at a different location or store. We see no sense in paying more for essentially the same product somewhere else. We, therefore, want them as cheaply as

What is a brand?

possible. A red apple is a red apple. Do you see where I'm headed?

Okay, keep this commodity situation in mind. We'll coming back to it in a moment.

Now, let's say that we bought a few red apples from the first grocery store and let's say that over the course of one week, ate and enjoyed them. They were delicious and we want more.

Uh, oh. We have a problem. Do you see it?

How will we be able to identify those exact red apples in the future? Huh. Right. There were no identifying marks. There was no name, another branding element, or logo attached to them. There was just a small bar code sticker.

In the future, we couldn't ask a clerk for those specific apples by name because there was none. Is the problem becoming clearer? Yeah.

Here is branding lesson number two: brands ensure that we can identify their products or services in the future by labeling them. In other cases, they help us *identify* their products by how they package them. Just think of the famous Coke bottle shape. That's an example of how brands use packaging to help us identify their products. That little blue box from Tiffany's is another example. The Tiffany blue, a patented color, is also another way we can identify a product. Yeah, see how that works?

Now, if we went to a different store, the problem would be even worse. Again, because there was no name attached to

THE CLIMB

those specific apples, we can't research them. We don't know where they were grown or the growing process. What if we have health issues and need apples that are free of harmful chemicals? We have no idea how those apples were grown. There literally was no story attached to them at the store. There was just a bin full of red apples. There were no branding elements - no name, no logo, no special packaging, and no signage.

Again, because these apples don't have any branding elements, they are commodities. And when something, or someone, is perceived as being the same as something else, we want it as cheaply as possible. That's why you're not getting paid what you're worth. You are seen as just another attorney, accountant, dentist, yoga instructor or what have you. Yeah, you're starting to get the picture now, right?

Perhaps you've experienced this phenomenon recently. Your home irrigation system says, "I quit". Who do you call? You don't know. You have never called an irrigation person before.

So, what do you do? Uh, you Google it or you head to your neighborhood Facebook group.

Google offers up a dizzying array of choices and your fellow neighbors offer their opinions and referrals. In both cases, you are offered names you've never heard. You write down a few and make some calls. You explain your problem to each person and quickly learn that you're not dealing with rocket science. It's a service any licensed irrigation person can fix. How do you decide on which person will get the job? Yeah, you look for a good price. Even if your decision is not based solely on price, price still plays a critical role.

Why?

That's because none of them are branded. There's nothing about any one of them that stands out. They all sound the same. You have no emotional connection to any of them. You just want the job done well.

As you may have already determined, professionals can be commodities as well. To consumers, all unbranded optometrists are, well, optometrists. They all received similar education and are licensed. In fact, they perform the exact same procedures.

Look, when Wal-Mart and Target offer optometry services, that's a clear sign that the industry has become a commodity - all players are the same. Again, when something is a commodity, what do you do? Yeah, you focus on price.

Consumers see all unbranded attorneys, musicians, and dentists, just to name a few, as being the same. To them, all accountants are just accountants and all public speakers are just public speakers. They are red apples. You are a red apple. We must change this fact.

MAKING THE BRAND
What if the red apples were grown no more than 100 miles away? What if the farmer used a filtered irrigation system and no harmful pesticides? Because their apples are locally grown and they are free of harmful chemicals, they call their apples Fresh and Free. Get it? Yeah, there's now a name.

Now when you visit the grocery store, you recognize their distinct colors, logo and signage and you can ask for them by

THE CLIMB

name no matter where you are. And because of their health benefits, you don't mind paying more - something you would never do for non-branded apples.

See where I'm going with this?

Each element I mentioned above, colors, logo, signage and name, are brand elements. No one element makes a brand. But, collectively, with a few more elements, a brand is formed.

Enough about apples. Let's begin the process of building you a powerful personal brand, step-by-step.

STEP 1: BRAND VALUES

CHAPTER 2

THE MAGNETIC FORCE

Why are we attracted to some personal brands and not others?

Why would a person who seems to exhibit questionable behavior be attractive?

Why do we follow certain celebrities on social media and become raving fans of certain authors?

Why are millions of "monsters" attracted to Lady Gaga or Beyonce's women's empowerment messages?

What is it that makes Tim Ferris, the human experiment machine, so interesting?

What accounts for the explosive growth of Podcaster Pat Flynn?

What makes a woman stand in line for hours just to chat with Cleo Wade?

Why is basketball great Lebron James so interesting to organizational and governmental leaders off the court?

What exactly is attracting us to them and others? What is this magnetic force? And, more importantly, is this magnetic force reserved just for a select few? Can ordinary people learn how to attract thousands or perhaps millions to their work?

THE CLIMB

Well, let's find out.

A LOOK BACKWARDS

In this chapter, you will learn exactly what that magnetic force is. More importantly, you will learn how to communicate, through your actions, in such a way that you automatically attract the right people. In other words, you, yes, you, can learn to attract the right people too.

I'm going to share with you how to do so right now.

Okay, think of a leader, during any time period, that you really admire.

This person can be living or dead and they can be from any area of life - politics, religion, sports, education, business, media or what have you. Really take a moment, pause, and think about who this person is that influences, or influenced, you in some significant way. Please, don't skip this simple exercise. Take a moment and think of this person.

Pause now and think of this person.

Welcome back.

So, do you have a specific person in mind? Good.

Now, what specific actions did this person take that drew you to them? There was something that they did or are doing that drew/draws you to them. What was that specific action or are those specific actions. Specificity is the key. Give it some serious thought.

Let me help you.

Did they lead a peaceful movement, like Martin Luther King, Jr.?

Was it them feeding the sick and poor like Mother Theresa?

Did they work their way from being a doorman to becoming a renowned entrepreneur and real estate investor like John Henry?

Was it their conscientious objection to going to war like Muhammad Ali?

Did they become a sports champion after overcoming a catastrophic injury or childhood ailment like Eddy the Eagle?

Did they start a highly successful business after being fired from their corporate job?

Do they provide clean water like Nick Teixeira?

Do they feed thousands of homeless people through a program that they established?

Was it the fact that they stood in front of an army tank in protest in China?

Did they change careers later in life like Vera Wang?

Was it their tenacity in building a successful business after several failures?

THE CLIMB

Did they bounce back after nearly losing a leg and their life like Amberly Lago?

Did they use natural methods to lose over 120 pounds and keep it off like Nique the "Thick Fit Queen"?

Are they community-oriented like real estate professional Matt James?

Think about this person and what drew/draws you to them. Write down those specific actions that that person took or is taking. Again, it's really important that you list the specific actions. Actions speak louder than words.

List these actions now. Do it. Don't skip this part. List the specific actions this person took that attracted you or is taking that attracts you.

Welcome back.

THE ATTRACTION FACTOR

Okay, when you study what exactly connected you with this person, you will inevitably find that their personal values is/was the attraction factor.

To be more succinct, you were attracted to their values in action. Dr. Martin Luther King, Jr. was about equal rights for all. It was clear, through his actions, what he stood for. And there were millions who were willing to stand with him. They were automatically attracted to his resolve. We will discuss why in a moment.

There is an American comedian, Sinbad, who refuses to use profanity in his routines. He attracts large crowds of people who prefer clean comedy.

Steve Jobs built the most beloved brand based on the core value of being different.

See, your values are about what you do, not about what you say. And, when others see your values in action, they become attracted to you. Get it?

WHY PERSONAL VALUES MATTER

Let me tell you why personal values are really important. When you are building your brand and expanding your reach, you will be a stranger to most people you encounter. The bigger you get the more strangers will come into your life.

As such, they are going to ask a critical question: who are you? You can only answer that question through your actions.

Your values will tell them who you are and whether they can trust you, or not, based upon your consistent actions.

This is worth repeating: Your values will tell them who you are and whether they can trust you, or not, based upon your consistent actions.

See, your personal values are a guide. They tell you what relationships to enter and which to exit. This is also true for your patients, clients, customers or fans. Your values tell them whether they want to enter a relationship with you.

THE CLIMB

That last statement is key. Again, your personal values tell them, your audience or tribe, whether it's safe to enter a relationship with you.

Of course, in most cases, they are not even aware of what's happening. They simply feel a certain way. Specifically, they feel safe.

If you are an actress, for example, who places your family above all else and you demonstrate these values in your media interviews, organizations you belong to, and protests you participate in, family oriented fans will flock to your book signings or personal appearances.

Is the picture becoming clear of how this whole thing works?

But, wait, there's more.

BECOME A BETTER DECISION MAKER

Knowing your values helps you make better decisions. They also help your audience or tribe make better decisions about who they will spend their time and money with.

When a controversial political issue arises, your core values will guide you in what stance you must take. If you don't take this stance, you will literally be unable to sleep or live with yourself, as some would say. That nagging feeling is your personal values speaking.

There are athletes, rappers, recording artists, comedians, and, yes, some politicians who will speak truth to power. It's not a game.

Professional football (American) player Colin Kaepernick decided to kneel during the playing of the national anthem to protest police brutality. There were millions who stood with him. Of course, there were millions who took offense to his stance and lodged their own protest.

The point is, by taking a stance, there were millions who stood with him. Whether you agree or disagree, the freedom to express such a view is aligned with American values.

There are businesspeople who will not sell certain products because of their core values. I recently heard of a shop owner who refused, for religious reasons, to make a cake for a gay couple who desired to get married. Again, people who share similar values are automatically attracted to such shop owners. Those who share the values of openness and tolerance are not.

Again, see how that works.

NOT ALL PERSONAL VALUES ARE FOR GOOD
Now, personal values are not just about something good. There are people who share values that are, well, questionable.

Some attorneys are known for walking close to the ethical and legal line. There are some clients who desire such services. They share the same values and are comfortable entering a relationship with people with questionable behavior. In fact, some even prefer working with people who walk, and sometimes cross over, the ethical and legal line.

Again, values dictate those relationships.

THE CLIMB

A quick note: if you've ever felt out of sorts on a job or in a relationship, it was because of a misalignment of values.

If a core value of yours is independence, for example, and you are required to work in teams, that will present a problem. You can make it work, but it won't be as comfortable as you are working alone. A smart manager or leader would allow you to work alone for long as possible and then have you join the group when final decisions are being made.

The bottom line is, your fans, patients, customers, or clients will be attracted to specific personal values. That's why personal values are the first step in the climb.

But first, you must know your values before you can live them fully. And that's what we will do next: help you to unearth your core values.

CHAPTER 3

YOUR PERSONAL VALUES

Your personal values tell your audience what you stand for. It is this stance that automatically attracts them to you. A bodybuilder who believes in natural muscle growth, for example, will automatically attract those who don't believe in taking steroids or other enhancements.

Remember, your personal values tell you what relationships to enter and which to exit. They affect your decisions. They are your compass. And thousands, and perhaps millions, are willing to follow your direction when you consistently live values that are congruent with theirs.

Let's talk about how you do that now.

PERSONAL VALUES EXERCISE
We are going to perform a simple but powerful exercise that will help you unearth your core values. I have provided you with a list of personal values at the back of this chapter.

Take a moment and refer to this list now.

Welcome back.

Now, refer to the list and circle or write down each personal value that appeals to you.

THE CLIMB

Don't limit yourself. Circle as many as you like. Remember, this is a feeling exercise, not a thinking one.

There are no right responses, per se. You can't game the system.

Again, circle all the personal values that appeal to you as you approach them.

Do that now.

Welcome back.

Now, count the number of personal values you've circled.

Okay, let's say you've circled or written down 63. That's perfectly okay. We will reduce them to a workable number.

Now, reduce this number, 63, 45, 81, or whatever it is, down to 25, if you have that many.

Reduce the number now. To be clear, when you are done, you should be left with 25 personal values. (Now, if you only selected, say, 24 values, then you would skip this portion and reduce your number, whatever it is, to 15.)

Ready? Go.

Welcome back.

Again, if you have 25 or more values, reduce these values to 15. Next, you will reduce these 15 personal values to five (5).

Pause and complete this task. Reduce whatever number you have down to five (5) values.

Welcome back.

The goal is to end up with five core values.

Here are my five core values:
Creativity
Entrepreneurship
Significance
Excellence
Education

Now, in my daily activities, I tend to work with three core values. I know some people who only work with one core value for a specified period of time - a week, month or year, even.

Here are a few examples of values in action.

Podcaster Pat Flynn
Podcaster Pat Flynn has amassed a huge following in a short period of time. One of the reasons is his wholesome, family-oriented style.

His social media bio, as of this writing, read as follows: I'm a father and husband who supports my family with passive income from online businesses.

If you listen to his Podcast, and I do, you will notice that his genuine family values come through. He mentions his family quite

THE CLIMB

frequently and he doesn't allow profane language on his show. He is always protecting his kids.

Even if you find his strict rule a little strange for today's time, his guests respect him. That's because that's who he is and he doesn't apologize. Neither should you.

Dave Ramsey

Next is personal finance guru Dave Ramsey. He values freedom - especially freedom from debt.

For Dave, freedom from debt brings peace, another core value. Perhaps that's why his main financial program is called Financial Peace University. By the way, he has sold hundreds of thousands of copies of his program. There are millions of people who resonate with these values.

Jonathan Fields

Jonathan Fields loves discovering stories. Discovery is a core value of his.

I'm sharing these with you to give you a quick picture of how personal values are often shared. Sometimes it is in a course like Financial Peace University and other times it is in blog posts. Sometimes personal values are reflected in Podcast episodes and other times during speeches at a podium.

Again, personal values are about action. They leave clues.

The point is, you must place your personal values into action. We will discuss how next.

PERSONAL VALUES WORKSHEET

Acceptance	Endurance	Hard work
Accountability	Energy	Harmony
Accuracy	Enjoyment	Health
Achievement	Enthusiasm	Honesty
Adaptability	Equality	Honor
Alertness	Ethical	Hope
Altruism	Excellence	Humility
Ambition	Experience	Imagination
Amusement	Exploration	Improvement
Assertiveness	Expressive	Independence
Attentive	Fairness	Individuality
Awareness	Family	Innovation
Balance	Famous	Inquisitive
Beauty	Fearless	Insightful
Boldness	Feelings	Inspiring
Bravery	Ferocious	Integrity
Brilliance	Fidelity	Intelligence
Calm	Focus	Intensity
Candor	Foresight	Intuitive
Capable	Fortitude	Irreverent
Careful	Freedom	Joy
Certainty	Friendship	Justice
Challenge	Fun	Kindness
Charity	Generosity	Knowledge
Cleanliness	Genius	Lawful
Clear	Giving	Leadership
Clever	Goodness	Learning
Drive	Grace	Liberty
Effectiveness	Gratitude	Logic
Efficiency	Greatness	Love
Empathy	Growth	Loyalty
Empower	Happiness	Mastery

THE CLIMB

Maturity
Meaning
Moderation
Motivation
Openness
Optimism
Order
Organization
Originality
Passion
Patience
Peace
Performance
Persistence
Playfulness
Poise
Potential
Power
Present
Productivity
Professionalism
Prosperity
Purpose
Quality
Realistic
Reason
Recognition
Recreation
Reflective
Respect
Responsibility
Restraint
Results-oriented
Reverence
Rigor
Risk
Satisfaction
Security
Self-reliance

Selfless
Sensitivity
Serenity
Service
Sharing
Significance
Silence
Simplicity
Sincerity
Skill
Skillfulness
Smart
Solitude
Spirit
Spirituality
Spontaneous
Stability
Status
Stewardship
Strength
Structure
Success
Support
Surprise
Sustainability
Talent
Teamwork
Temperance
Thankful
Thorough
Thoughtful
Timeliness
Tolerance
Toughness
Traditional
Tranquility
Transparency
Trust
Trustworthy
Truth

Understanding
Uniqueness
Unity
Valor
Victory
Vigor
Vision
Vitality
Wealth
Welcoming
Winning
Wisdom
Wonder

CHAPTER 4

YOUR VALUES IN ACTION

Now that you have identified your five core values, it's time to place them into action.

First, review the examples I offered in the last section. But don't limit yourself to those. As you come across personal brands, ask, how are they conveying their personal values? Of course, it will be a guess in some cases and in others it will be obvious what they stand for. Lady Gaga stands for tolerance and creative expression. Her dress and songs reflect these values. They are obvious.

Next, begin mapping out how you will infuse your personal values into your life. Now, if you already are, bravo. If you can do better or haven't done them at all, here are a few suggestions:

Review your profile pic, about page, blog posts and other material. If you don't have any of these, then you can still use these suggestions when you do. For example, review your blog posts. Is it evident what you stand for by reading your posts? If integrity is a core value, do you use your posts to demonstrate integrity? Again, your values are about what you do, not what you say.

HOW TO BECOME MORE MAGNETIC

Okay, here's what I suggest: Pick one personal value and focus on it for a week.

Let's say that you are a photographer and you have as a core value education - education in terms of teaching.

Plan, right now, how you will infuse that value in your life.

So, for example, you might begin educating your audience, through Tweets and Facebook posts, about the process for selecting a wedding photographer.

When couples are getting married, there are lots of questions about the vows, venues, catering, and more. One important overriding question is about the photographer. Someone must capture those wonderful moments.

Now, as a photographer, you can take a leadership role by helping couples with this important issue.

You can, for example, tweet and post the top 10 questions couples must ask before selecting a wedding photographer. Good wedding photographers can be expensive and difficult to select.

Then you plan out ten individual Tweets and posts with each question. Got that?

Next, you Tweet and post each question one-by-one over several days. Maybe one question a day on several platforms and double up during high traffic times. So, you would post the question a couple might ask on Twitter, Facebook, Instagram, and

Pinterest. On day two of your campaign, you will post another question on these platforms.

Got it?

CONNECTING WITH YOUR AUDIENCE

Here's the deal: as you consistently post educational items, your audience will come to expect and enjoy these posts. They will share them and tell others about the valuable information that you provide. Your name will get mentioned thousands of times. When they or others begin seeking a photographer, you will become one that they will consider.

See how that works?

Let's do another one. In this case, let's say the core value you will focus on is peace. Of course, peace can be manifested in many ways. But, being a photographer, you want to share what peace means to you. It might be a beautiful ocean or the absence of war. On social media, you might post images of oceans, yoga poses, flowers, children or what have you. Or, you might show photos of some form of solidarity among traditional enemies.

The key is to place your core value into action. Start living it.

Now, if a core value is, say, leadership and you don't have several posts about leadership, you have work to do. First, define what leadership means to you. How is it represented?

So, how long will it take before your audience begins connecting with you? I have no idea and if anyone says that they know, they are flat out lying.

THE CLIMB

Look, I can't predict your efforts. Here's what I do know: if you only post one Tweet, it will not move the needle. At a minimum, you need to post and Tweet for at least 30 days straight. Others will suggest shorter or longer periods of time. Again, it depends upon your area of expertise, where you are now in the market, and where you're trying to go. The point is, Tweet, post, update your profile pic, and perform other branding activities that are values-oriented regularly. Eventually, you will see great results.

A FINAL NOTE ABOUT PERSONAL VALUES

Your values tell the world what you stand for. What you are willing to fight for. Remember, this stance is what's attractive to your audience. The goal, then, is to share with the world through all your activities what you stand for. If you stand for family, then your profile pic, blog posts, speeches, books, videos and other touchpoints should reflect this reality.

For example, to basketball superstar Steph Curry, family and faith are important. So, you won't hear stories about him going to night clubs or showing off his wealth. He would rather watch a movie with his wife and kids. Again, he lives his values and millions are attracted to him for this and many other reasons.

Remember, this is the first step in you telling your story.

But there is another nugget for knowing and living your values. See, people need a reason to follow you, vote for you, or buy your music or products. They need a reason why. Your personal values give them a reason to believe. They give them a reason to listen to you. They give them a reason to buy you. Get it?

Your Values in Action

Your values are your way of sharing ownership with your audience. You're telling them that "we are one". We get each other.

It's absolutely essential that you know your values and live them.

STEP 2: YOUR BRAND STORY

CHAPTER 5

YOUR BRAND STORY

Everything about this book is customer, client, patient, prospect, or fan focused. I wrote this book from their perspective, not yours.

Here's why: In the end, when you brand, and you do it effectively, the customer will tell you the value of your brand. They will tell you whether your efforts are connecting. They will do this by buying and reading your books, visiting your blog, listening to your speeches, attending your yoga classes, ordering your consulting report, or seeking your legal advice.

Now, when a client or prospect engages your brand, they do so because they have some expectation, some outcome, or some result in mind.

They want to know, specifically, if you can solve their problem or alleviate their pain or frustration. They want to know if you can reduce their stress.

They want to know if you can help them get through buying their first home without all the stress that goes along with it.

They want to know if your fitness program will help them become skinnier, bigger, or stronger.

THE CLIMB

They want to know if you can help alleviate their back pain without the use of surgery.

They want to know if your book will help them sell more computers.

They want an authentic connection with you.

Okay, so, how do you do this? How do you introduce yourself to them in such a way that they feel a connection with you? After all, powerful brands, whether products or people, make us feel a certain way, right?

IT'S ALL ABOUT THE STORY, MAN

One of the best ways to introduce yourself and begin the process of making that connection is through your brand story.

Your story is how you demonstrate to prospects and reinforce with clients that you get them; that you understand their pain. That's because you have experienced the same or a similar problem. If you haven't, you demonstrated that you have helped many like them and you share how you have through your story.

TWO BIG QUESTIONS

Your story will answer two questions all new prospects will have about you: who are you and why are you here? Again, who are you and why are you here?

These are two powerful psychological questions. The first asks, are you credible and can you be trusted? The second asks, do you understand my problems (pain, fear, or frustration) and can you solve them?

Are you credible? Can you be trusted? Do you understand my problems? More importantly, can you help solve them?

See, a compelling story answers all these questions. Note that I wrote a compelling story. A compelling story. Yup.

NOT ALL STORIES ARE CREATED EQUAL

The fact of the matter is, you don't want to tell just any story. No, that's a complete waste of time. You want to tell a compelling story. That means that there's a difference between a regular story and a compelling one.

True, a regular story might make you think. But a compelling story will make you act. Yeah. Big difference.

So, we're going to help you discover your story and turn that story into a compelling story.

THE COMPELLING STORY

But, first, what makes a compelling story, a compelling story? In other words, how do you tell a story in way that it connects emotionally with your audience? After all, if you don't connect emotionally, you can't move them. So, let's begin the process by first understanding what a compelling story really is. And, the best way to understand compelling stories is to study them. To do that we're going to deconstruct them, create a template and apply that template to your story.

Cool? Cool.

For this reason, we're going to discuss three stories that we already know to be compelling: Snow White, The Shawshank Redemption and Toms Shoes brand story.

THE CLIMB

I use these three stories to demonstrate that a compelling story has the same structure regardless of genre or format. It doesn't matter if it's a fictional cartoon character or a real-life brand story. A compelling story is a compelling story.

Because I'm not going to assume that you know the fairytale Snow White, the movie Shawshank Redemption, or the Toms Shoes band story, I have included a synopsis of all three for you to review.

Pause for a moment and review these stories. Doing so will give you some insight into this process. Next, we're going to review, in detail, the anatomy of a compelling story.

STORY SYNOPSIS

THE SHAWSHANK REDEMPTION SYNOPSIS

In 1947 Portland, Maine, banker Andy Dufresne is convicted of murdering his wife and her lover and sentenced to two consecutive life sentences at the Shawshank State Penitentiary. He is befriended by contraband smuggler, Ellis "Red" Redding, an inmate serving a life sentence. Red procures a rock hammer, and later a large poster of Rita Hayworth for Andy. Working in the prison laundry, Andy is regularly assaulted and raped by "the Sisters" and their leader, Bogs.

In 1949, Andy overhears the captain of the guards, Byron Hadley, complaining about being taxed on an inheritance and offers to help him shelter the money legally. After an assault by the Sisters nearly kills Andy, Hadley beats Bogs severely. Left crippled, Bogs is transferred to another prison, and Andy is not attacked again. Warden Samuel Norton meets Andy and reassigns him to the prison library to assist elderly inmate Brooks Hatlen. Andy's new job is a pretext for him to begin managing financial matters for the prison employees. As time passes, the warden begins using him to handle matters for himself and a variety of people, including guards from other prisons. Andy begins writing weekly letters to the state legislature requesting funds to improve the prison's decaying library.

Brooks is paroled in 1954 after serving 50 years, but he cannot adjust to the outside world, and he commits suicide by hanging himself. Andy receives a library donation that includes a recording of The Marriage of Figaro. He plays an excerpt over the public address system and is punished with solitary confinement. After his release from solitary, Andy explains that hope is what gets him through his time, a concept that Red dismisses. In 1963, Norton begins exploiting prison labor for

THE CLIMB

public works, profiting by undercutting skilled labor costs and receiving bribes. Andy launders the money using the alias Randall Stephens.

Tommy Williams is incarcerated for burglary in 1965. Andy and Red befriend him, and Andy helps him pass his GED exam. A year later, Tommy reveals to Red and Andy that an inmate at another prison claimed responsibility for the murders for which Andy was convicted. Andy approaches Norton with this information, but he refuses to listen and sends him back to solitary confinement when he mentions the money laundering. Norton has Hadley murder Tommy under the guise of an escape attempt. Andy declines to continue the laundering, but he relents after Norton threatens to burn the library, remove Andy's protection from the guards, and move him to worse conditions. After two months, Andy is released from solitary confinement, and he tells Red of his dream of living in Zihuatanejo, a Mexican coastal town. Red feels Andy is being unrealistic, but promises him that if he is ever released, he will visit a specific hayfield near Buxton, Maine, and retrieve a package Andy buried there. He worries about Andy's well-being, especially when he learns Andy asked another inmate to supply him with six feet (1.8 meters) of rope.

The next day at roll call, the guards find Andy's cell empty. An irate Norton throws a rock at the poster of Raquel Welch hanging on the cell wall, revealing a tunnel that Andy dug with his rock hammer over the last 19 years. The previous night, Andy escaped through the tunnel and prison sewage pipe, using the rope to bring with him Norton's suit, shoes, and the ledger containing details of the money laundering. While guards search for him, Andy poses as Randall Stephens and visits several banks to withdraw the laundered money, then mails the ledger and evidence of the corruption and murders at Shawshank to a local newspaper. State police arrive at Shawshank and take Hadley into custody, while Norton commits suicide to avoid arrest.

The Shawshank Redemption

After serving 40 years, Red is paroled. He struggles to adapt to life outside prison and fears that he never will. Remembering his promise to Andy, he visits Buxton and finds a cache containing money, and a letter asking him to come to Zihuatanejo. Red violates his parole and travels to Fort Hancock, Texas, to cross the border into Mexico, admitting he finally feels hope. On a beach in Zihuatanejo he finds Andy, and the two friends are happily reunited.

Source: Wikipedia

SNOW WHITE STORY SYNOPSIS

Snow White is a lonely princess living with her stepmother, a vain Queen. The Queen worries that Snow White will look better than her, so she forces Snow White to work as a scullery maid and asks her Magic Mirror daily "who is the fairest one of all". For years the mirror always answered that the Queen was, pleasing her.

One day, the Magic Mirror informs the Queen that Snow White is now "the fairest" in the land. The jealous Queen orders her Huntsman to take Snow White into the forest and kill her. She further demands that the huntsman return with Snow White's heart in a jeweled box as proof of the deed. However, the Huntsman cannot bring himself to kill Snow White. He tearfully begs for her forgiveness, revealing the Queen wants her dead and urges her to flee into the woods and never look back. Lost and frightened, the princess is befriended by woodland creatures who led her to a cottage deep in the woods. Finding seven small chairs in the cottage's dining room, Snow White assumes the cottage is the untidy home of seven orphaned children.

In reality, the cottage belongs to seven adult dwarfs, named Doc, Grumpy, Happy, Sleepy, Bashful, Sneezy, and Dopey, who work in a nearby mine. Returning home, they are alarmed to find their cottage clean and suspect that an intruder has invaded their home. The dwarfs find Snow White upstairs, asleep across three of their beds. Snow White awakes to find the dwarfs at her bedside

THE CLIMB

and introduces herself, and all the dwarfs eventually welcome her into their home after they she offers to clean and cook for them. Snow White keeps house for the dwarfs while they mine for jewels during the day, and at night they all sing, play music and dance.

Meanwhile, the Queen discovers that Snow White is still alive when the mirror again answers that Snow White is the fairest in the land and reveals that the heart in the jeweled box is that of a pig. Using a potion to disguise herself as an old hag, the Queen creates a poisoned apple that will put whoever eats it into the "Sleeping Death", a curse she learns can only be broken by "love's first kiss", but is certain Snow White will be buried alive. While the Queen goes to the cottage while the dwarfs are away, the animals are wary of her and rush off to find the dwarfs. Faking a potential heart attack, the Queen tricks Snow White into bringing her into the cottage to rest. The Queen fools Snow White into biting into the poisoned apple under the pretense that it is a magic apple that grants wishes. As Snow White falls asleep the Queen proclaims that she is now the fairest of the land. The dwarfs return with the animals as the Queen leaves the cottage and give chase, trapping her on a cliff. She tries to roll a boulder over them, but before she can do so, lightning strikes the cliff, causing her to fall to her death.

The dwarfs return to their cottage and find Snow White seemingly dead, being kept in a deathlike slumber by the poison. Unwilling to bury her out of sight in the ground, they instead place her in a glass coffin trimmed with gold in a clearing in the forest. Together with the woodland creatures, they keep watch over her.

A year later, a prince, who had previously met and fallen in love with Snow White, learns of her eternal sleep and visits her coffin. Saddened by her apparent death, he kisses her, which breaks the spell and awakens her. The dwarfs and animals all rejoice as the Prince takes Snow White to his castle.

Source: Wikipedia/Disney

TOMS SHOES ORIGIN STORY

In 2006, while in Argentina, Blake Mycoskie noticed that children weren't wearing shoes.

As a result, blisters, sores and cuts were on their feet.

Of course, this can lead to infection.

He returned to L.A. and vowed to do something about this issue.

Being an entrepreneur, he did what entrepreneurs do. He discovered a problem and formed a business to solve it.

That's when he founded a company that eventually became Toms Shoes.

Toms Shoes is a for profit company.

However, to help these children and others around the world, he did something a little different. For every pair of shoes that he sold, he would give one pair away.

To date, Toms Shoes has given away over 40 million pairs of shoes.

Okay, what we're going to do now is go deeper into what made his story interesting and the two others that you have read.

CHAPTER 6

ANATOMY OF A COMPELLING STORY

We've established that there's a difference between an ordinary story and a compelling story. But what really makes a story compelling? And, is it possible to build a compelling story framework that you can use? We will answer both questions now.

First, be prepared to take copious notes. We're going into great detail about what makes a story compelling. There are lots of moving parts and I don't want you to miss anything. Let's go.

COMPELLING STORY STRUCTURE

1. MAIN CHARACTER

The first thing to note is that each story has a main character and, in some cases, characters.

Snow White is, of course, a main character. But I would argue that the wicked stepmother is also a main character. Besides, without the wicked stepmother, the story is not as interesting.

In the Shawshank Redemption, Andy Dufrense is a main character. So, is Red. We might even say that the jail is a main

THE CLIMB

character. A main character, therefore, doesn't have to be a human being.

Blake Mycoskie is the main character of Toms Shoes. But so are the shoes. Again, a main character can be a shoe, jail or cartoon character. The main characters in Finding Nemo, for example, are Nemo and Dori. They are both fish.

2. THE SETTING/SITUATION

The next element that makes a story is the setting or situation that the main character or characters find themselves in.

Snow white is the daughter of a king who marries a woman. This woman, of course, becomes Snow White's stepmother. It must be a stepmother, right? It's difficult to imagine one's own mother being so ruthless. Sorry. I digress.

Anyway, her stepmother has an interesting habit of asking a magical mirror who is the fairest, most beautiful, of them all. The mirror always says it is she. Ah, that's until Snow White grows older and more beautiful. Uh oh.

Soon, the mirror, when asked, doesn't say that the stepmother is the most beautiful. It says Snow White is. What? "Yeah, girl, you've been replaced," I can hear the mirror saying.

"Oh, hell no," I can hear the stepmother responding. LOL!

Okay, back to the story. The fact that the stepmother is no longer the fairest drives her nuts. This is the situation that sets up the rest of the story.

On to The Shawshank Redemption. Here, Andy Dufresne is a banker who is convicted of murdering his wife and her lover. In the beginning of the movie, we don't know if he's innocent or guilty. Nevertheless, he is given a life sentence and sent to Shawshank State Prison. That's the Shawshank situation.

Finally, Toms Shoes. Blake Mycoskie is on a trip in Argentina having lunch with volunteers. He notices the children are not wearing shoes. This fact means that they can't attend school. He vows to do something about it.

There you have them. Three different situations for three different stories.

3. THE STRUGGLE

Every compelling story has an element of struggle, some great problem, frustration or pain. That statement is worth repeating. Every compelling story, and I mean every, has an element of struggle, some great problem, frustration or pain.

It's this struggle, frustration, pain or some problem that makes a story a compelling story. Make note of this fact.

Again, without a struggle or some tension the story is just a regular story. Get the difference? Again, regular stories don't have the element of drama or pain. Compelling stories do. Got it? Cool.

For example, Snow White, the story, became interesting when the stepmother vowed to kill her.

Andy Dufrense was regularly taken advantage of (raped) by a gang of men. He was mistreated by the guards and prison warden. And there were other struggles. But all these struggles made the movie compelling. It made his escape interesting. There's no need to escape from heaven, right?

Blake Mycoskie had to figure out how to make enough profit to keep his promise of giving away a pair of shoes for each that they sold. It wasn't as simple as it sounded. Many people provide services for children. But it was the way he helped, by building a company, that made it interesting.

New York Times Bestselling author and television personality Suze Orman definitely had her share of problems. She was a waitress who had raised $50,000 to open a restaurant. She invested the money with a Merrill Lynch broker who lost it all. This loss fueled her financial advisory career. Without this major setback, she's probably an unknown restaurateur.

Jillian Michaels, television personality and fitness expert, was bullied as a child for being overweight.

The point is, behind every powerful personal brand is some struggle. The person may not have personally experienced the pain, but they were close enough to be affected by it. An example is Nancy Brinker, the sister of Susan Komen. She watched her sister succumb to breast cancer and vowed to do something about it.

Now this is key: when a prospect, client, customer, patient or fan believes that you get them, that you understand their problems, they are attracted to you like a moth to a flame.

Did you get that?

Please don't miss this point. It's this shared struggle that connects you to them. Remember, earlier in the book, we said that branding

Anatomy of a Compelling Story

was about connection and you connect with your audiences through your story. This struggle is specifically how you connect with them.

4. THE ACTION

Each main character took some action that solved the problem, alleviated the pain, or frustration.

Snow White was awakened by the kiss of the prince. Okay, she didn't take the action, but the prince did. The point is, some action was taken.

Andy Dufresne, with the help of Red, planned his escape from Shawshank by chipping away at the cement wall over a twenty-year period.

Blake Mycoskie started a company.

One of the founders of Warby-Parker, the fast-growing eyeware company, couldn't afford to replace his eyeglasses. He even went a semester in graduate school without them. This frustration, the cost of replacement, led to them founding the company.

In each case, there was some action that was taken to alleviate the pain or solve a problem.

5. THE RESOLUTION

Then there is some resolution. In other words, the problem is being solved or is resolved through specific actions.

The wicked stepmother finds her demise after Snow White marries the prince.

THE CLIMB

Andy Dufresne ends up with the warden's money and lands on a beach in Mexico. Red soon joins him.

Toms Shoes delivers over 40 million pairs of shoes.

We can go on and on.

PERSONAL VALUES IN ACTION

So, there we have it. The main character, the situation, the struggle, some action and resolution.

Now, note how one's values influence decisions in each story. The wicked stepmother valued beauty and being the most beautiful.

Andy Dufresne valued integrity and freedom.

Blake Mycoskie valued children and their overall health. Entrepreneurship is also a core value of his.

Suze Orman valued knowledge.

See, this stuff works.

Now, on to a few story examples.

CHAPTER 7

STORY EXAMPLES

The best way to get a feel for this model and to eventually construct your own story is to review examples of compelling brand stories.

Some are more compelling than others. Nevertheless, they all follow the model or framework I've provided for you. Let's review them now.

SEEING CLEARLY

The first story is that of the fast-growing eyewear company Warby Parker.

Here's Warby Parker's story from their website:

"Every idea starts with a problem. Ours was simple: glasses are too expensive. We were students when one of us lost his glasses on a backpacking trip. The cost of replacing them was so high that he spent the first semester of grad school without them, squinting and complaining. (We don't recommend this.) The rest of us had similar experiences, and we were amazed at how hard it was to find a pair of great frames that didn't leave our wallets bare. Where were the options?

It turns out there was a simple explanation. The eyewear industry is dominated by a single company that has been able to keep prices artificially high while reaping huge profits from consumers who have no other options.

THE CLIMB

We started Warby Parker to create an alternative.

By circumventing traditional channels, designing glasses in-house, and engaging with customers directly, we're able to provide higher-quality, better-looking prescription eyewear at a fraction of the going price.

We believe that buying glasses should be easy and fun. It should leave you happy and good-looking, with money in your pocket.

We also believe that everyone has the right to see.

Almost one billion people worldwide lack access to glasses, which means that 15% of the world's population cannot effectively learn or work. To help address this problem, Warby Parker partners with non-profits like VisionSpring to ensure that for every pair of glasses sold, a pair is distributed to someone in need.

There's nothing complicated about it. Good eyewear, good outcome."

ANALYSIS OF THE WARBY-PARKER STORY

Okay, first, note that all the elements of a compelling story are present.

You have characters, the two founders. I would also say that the industry is a character.

Then you have a situation of one of them losing his glasses on a backpacking trip. The industry is also dominated by a single player.

Next, he states the problem: he couldn't afford to replace his glasses and goes through the entire semester of graduate school without them. I wear glasses and I can't even imagine not being able to see clearly for that length of time. It is painful.

They also learn that the industry is controlled by a major player who keeps the prices artificially high.

But they take a specific action: they start a company that offers high quality eyewear at an affordable price.

Starting this company though, is driven by their core values - probably fairness and social entrepreneurship.

They have raised millions of dollars from investors and the company is valued at over a billion dollars.

By the way, like Toms Shoes, they too give away a pair of glasses for each that they sell.

Now, one of the reasons they have received so much media attention is their story. And they are good at telling it. But when they do, they always use this exact model. So, can you. But you must discover your story first. And that's what we're going to do next.

CHAPTER 8

DISCOVERING YOUR STORY

I'm going to go through the process of helping you tell your compelling story. But you can't tell a story that you don't know. Therefore, you must first discover your story. This means two things: One, your story already exists, and, two, discovery is about asking questions.

I will ask a few questions to help you get going. Let's get started right now.

First, grab your five core values. As I stated before, your values will permeate every aspect of your brand, as we saw with the examples I provided earlier. They will play a special role in the action section of your story.

Take a moment to retrieve your list of core values.

Next, think of a situation, whether at work, in your personal life, or some recreational activity, where you experienced or was a part of some significant setback, obstacle, pain, problem or frustration.

It could be an insurance process in your dental practice that sucked up your staff's time and made life hard for your patients.

THE CLIMB

It could have been a necessary software package that continuously crashed.

It could have been you caring for a loved one who is battling cancer.

It could have been you dealing with a child who was/is drug dependent.

Describe in detail the situation. Remember, the situation is about the who, what, when and where. Who was involved? Meaning, your characters, if you will. What was happening? When did this all take place? Where did this happen?

Next, describe, in detail, the problem, pain, frustration, stress or obstacle you faced in this situation. For example, the insurance process caused you to hire extra help at significant cost. And, you lost patients who grew sick of the convoluted paperwork.

Or, the software package caused you to lose three clients in one week. One client even threatened to sue you. Your business was on the brink of collapse.

Or, you had to watch your loved one go through the pain of receiving chemo and losing their hair and a significant amount of weight. And, you experienced the loneliness of a caretaker.

A quick note before we move on. Problems, pain or frustration tend to originate from three sources: People, products and processes. In other words, there are people problems, product problems, and process problems.

Once you have described the problem, think about the specific action that you took to overcome this pain, frustration, problem or stress.

For example, did you end up writing and publishing a book?

Did you create a drug dependency program?

Did you create a blog and a support group for caretakers?

Did you have a software solution developed that reduced staff time?

Did you create an accounting process that saves clients at least 12%?

VALUES IN ACTION
Your personal values are about your actions, right? So, your actions should be indicative of your personal values. What if a core value of yours is entrepreneurship? You might have, for example, started a company to raise funds for cancer research. Remember, this was one of the specific actions that Blake Mycoskie took with Toms Shoes.

THE RESULTS ARE IN
Finally, list the result or resolution. In other words, what ended up happening after your action?

Did the teen gain control of the drug problem?

Did your book become a bestseller and touch the lives of thousands?

THE CLIMB

Did you improve the lives of caregivers by sharing stories via FaceBook, Instagram, or on your blog?

Sometimes things don't work out. You must go back to the drawing board. If so, share that aspect of your story.

STORY TIME: THE JOB INTERVIEW
By the way, this model or framework is extremely effective when interviewing for a position.

Inevitably, the job interviewer will ask you to share an example or two of your strengths. In other words, demonstrate how you made things happen. This model of describing the situation, the struggle, your action and the results or resolution works. I've personally used this model in the past and I have been told by organizations like Johnson & Johnson, Ernst & Young, Amgen and others that it was my painting of this picture that captured them.

PUT IT ON PAPER
I strongly recommend that you write out the people involved, or characters, the situation, the struggle, the action you took, and the result or resolution.

See, writing reveals flaws. So, write it. Don't expect perfection. Write it and rewrite. Rewrite it again.

Finally, remember, discovering and sharing your story take time. It is rare for one to construct a story that resonates on the first try. As such, practice, practice, practice. Then share your story with at least three people.

Now, this next suggestion is important. Tell them that you are developing your story and you want to know how to improve it. If you offered it to them without telling them that it is in development, they will always give you a positive answer. No one wants to rain on your parade.

That's it. There is no magic bullet. The story will not fall out of the sky. You must go through the process. If you are not satisfied with your story, rewrite it. Share it. Get feedback. Again, this and no system is perfect. But it works. Just look at all the stories we've discussed.

Lastly, I will share with you where to share your story. Of course, one place is your about page on your website or blog. But there are many other places to share your story. We will cover them as we go along.

STEP 3: BRAND POSITIONING

CHAPTER 9

BRAND POSITIONING INTRODUCTION

As an author, trainer, consultant, coach, or other expert, you live in a noisy world. Each year, new words are added to our lexicon and new products sit on top of the thousands that already occupy our minds. In fact, it is estimated that the average consumer is exposed to about 6,000 or more marketing messages every day.

I have no idea if this number is high, low or somewhere in between. Here's what I do know. Just 15 years ago (as of this writing in 2019), words, apps, and products like FaceBook, Twitter, iPads, iPhones, Pinterest, SnapChat, and Instagram didn't even exist. Some didn't exist five years ago.

So, yeah, no matter what industry you're in, you are faced with a unique dilemma. See, you're not just competing with people, products, and companies in your space, you are competing with the excessive noise in the entire marketplace.

And, it gets worse. Today's consumers are so overwhelmed with information that they don't want to hear from anyone about anything. If it sounds or looks like a sales pitch of any kind, they immediately tune out.

Ah, but there is one major exception: they eagerly listen to those who can address their unique problems. If you have a toothache, for example, you are open to anyone who can help. In

THE CLIMB

some cases, you actively seek help. But, those are emergency situations and most situations aren't emergencies. Still, consumers will respond, at some level, to those who address issues they are seeking to solve.

Now, as a personal brand, it gets tricky. See, you must be able to communicate that you can solve their problems. You must stand out enough to gain their attention. Otherwise, you will be adding to the already deafening noise. And you don't want to do that. In that case, no one wins.

HOW TO STAND OUT

Okay, so how do you stand out? How do you break through this noise? How do you get them to pay attention? How do you get them to at least listen?

Great questions, right?

Well, that's where positioning comes in.

Positioning literally means placing your product, service, idea, or your person in a specific location in the minds of consumers. In other words, when you position yourself, you own a piece of real estate in the minds of consumers.

Let me break positioning down even further.

Okay, think of your hometown. The size of your town or city doesn't matter - although a larger city would bring greater clarity to the exercise.

In my case, I'm thinking of downtown Charlotte, North Carolina. It's where my family currently resides.

Brand Positioning Intro

Charlotte is like any other city. There are tall buildings throughout downtown. Of course, there are stadiums and parks too. And there are single family homes and townhouses throughout.

Now, picture your town or city. If you're able to access a photo of it on your phone, tablet, computer, or other method, do so now.

Pay attention to all the buildings that you see. Pick one in the foreground. In other words, one that is closest to you in the photo. Such a structure is easier to see from the ground up.

Now, wherever you see a building, just think, no other building can occupy that space without first tearing the original down. If a building is already there, you can't place another on top of it without first removing the existing structure. That's common sense, right?

Note that each building is *positioned* in a specific location, with a specific address.

Well, positioning, in terms of branding, is like a building occupying a specific location. Once a brand owns a location in the minds of consumers, no other brand can occupy that space. Get it? That's worth repeating. Once a brand owns a location in the minds of consumers, no other brand can occupy that space.

So, once you become the "vegan bodybuilding trainer", no one else can occupy that position; at least not in your area. Some brands are local, and others are global.

Here's what I mean about owning a position in the minds of consumers.

THE CLIMB

A SAFE ON WHEELS

Older Volvo cars were boxy, in terms of their shape. They looked sturdy. That shape told a story, though. And the story was, you and your family will be *safe* in here.

One of the strongest psychological needs is to protect our young, family, and property. As you can imagine, a big concern for those toting around precious human cargo is safety. And, *safety* was the piece of real estate Volvo owned.

Cool. But, how did Volvo do it? How did they win or own this position in the minds of consumers?

First, Volvo focused on building the world's safest cars. Again, you can't build a brand or position with a product that's not credible. The executive at Volvo understood this fact and focused on safety. So much so that a series of safety innovations followed.

Here are a few innovations Volvo brought to market:
- The three-point seatbelt
- Rear-facing child seat
- Lamda Sond, which reduced harmful exhaust emissions by 90%
- Side Impact Protection
- Whiplash Protection
- Roll-over Protection
- Inflatable Curtain
- And, more.

Yeah, you can thank Volvo for protecting you even if you don't own a Volvo.

Brand Positioning Intro

Granted, all these innovations occurred over decades. Still, Volvo established early on that they would occupy the safety position.

Here's how: Volvo ran television and print ads demonstrating each new safety feature. Their ads featured a family walking away unharmed after an accident. They shared their latest safety innovations as they developed them. With so much emphasis on safety, Volvo eventually owned the safety position in the auto market.

So, when consumers thought of purchasing a car that would protect their family, they literally thought of Volvo first.

See how that works?

This focus on safety worked for two reasons: one, Volvo was the first and only company to focus exclusively on safety. And, two, they could back up their claims.

For some inexplicable reason, however, Volvo backed off that positioning and began focusing on other attributes like speed. Yeah, they even featured an ad comparing their cars, in terms of speed, to a Ferrari. No kidding. They screwed it up.

By slowly demolishing their "safety building" with plans of erecting a new one, speed, for example, they cleared the land for other automakers to sneak in and build their own safety position.

Today, pretty much all cars are thought of as being safe. So, who owns the safety position today? Actually, no automaker does. And, that includes Volvo.

THE CLIMB

Yep, Volvo blew it.

Here's another classic example. As we established earlier, most people would say that BMW belongs to the luxury car category. This labeling makes sense, right? They compete head-to-head with Mercedes, Audi, and others.

Again, when you study their marketing and branding efforts, you will find something very interesting: you can't find the word luxury anywhere. They don't use that word in their radio, print, online or television marketing.

Why?

The smart people at BMW understand positioning. They know that trying to own the word luxury is impossible. Besides, that's not what their cars are about anyway. Their cars are about the drive.

Here's what I mean. Their cars handle corners beautifully thus making them fun to drive. Their cars really are fun to drive. And that's the point. BMW cars are about the driving experience.

Today, BMW owns the driving experience position. In fact, BMW is not shy about saying that they don't make cars. They make *ultimate driving machines*. Yup, ultimate driving machines; not the safest machines or the most luxurious machines. They make ultimate *driving* machines.

To reinforce this positioning, every non-car activity is also about the driving experience. When they support the Susan B. Komen breast cancer foundation, for example, they call their program, *The Drive for the Cure*. There goes that word *drive* again. See how they tied their brand position to that event? Nice.

Here are a few personal brand examples.

Dr. Oz owns, in terms of medical television personalities, *authentic health information.*

While Oz has been accused of getting close to "the ethical line" by some medical professionals, his tribe doesn't see it that way. They believe that he's there to give them the "truth". When a debate rose about arsenic in apple juice, one television personality sided with the apple juice industry taking on Oz directly. Consumers sided with Oz. That personality is no longer on television. Oz is.

To reinforce the notion that he offers authentic health information, Oz spends time at the end of each show debunking nefarious ads promising all sorts of cures. By calling out these dubious claims, Oz sends a message that he will always protect his audience.

Michael Hyatt touts himself as the *virtual mentor*. His logo is a compass. Mentors give direction, after all. See how these branding elements tie nicely together.

Sonny Webster, an Olympic weightlifter from Sydney, Australia, is the "Barbell Specialist".

Pat Flynn is about *transparency* when it comes to Internet marketing. Transparency is important when dealing with Internet marketers. Internet marketers are notorious for making claims that they never or can't substantiate. They take photos and shoot videos in from of borrowed private jets and exotic cars.

THE CLIMB

Flynn took this weakness of the industry and made it a strength. He posts his income and expenses for each month on his website. Each report, which anyone can access, is very extensive and detailed. He tells you where his income came from and how much he makes from each line item. Then he shares his expenses and net total with full explanations of each. He is transparent.

Now, this is cool. See, Pat sharing so much detail is indicative of one of his personal values - integrity. Yeah, this stuff all goes together.

Dave Ramsey was the first to successfully position himself as the debt elimination guy. And it has stuck. Today, when you perform a Google search on debt elimination, Ramsey's name is sure to pop up on the first page. This is the power of positioning.

There is one other thing about Ramsey: his Christian values. They permeate every aspect of his work. For example, one of his core values, peace, is at the center of his work. Besides, debt elimination brings you peace, right? In fact, his bestselling course *Financial Peace University* is the centerpiece of financial education at thousands of churches.

Again, see how this ties together?

Chef Sean Sherman grew up on a reservation in South Dakota. He *specializes in Native American food* -- specifically the pre-reservation foods of the Dakota and Ojibwe people who lived on the Great Plains. "I'm trying to really stay true to a lot of the indigenous ingredients as much as possible," he says. While that is a very narrow position, there are more than enough people in the United States, especially, who enjoy this type cuisine. And, his narrow positioning gets him lots of press.

Ariel Adams was the *first full-time watch blogger* after founding aBlogtoWatch in September of 2007. Being first helped cement his position in what is now a crowded field. Will he be able to maintain this position for long? Frankly, I'm not sure. You can only use being first for a limited period. Soon, some other positioning may overtake his (in the minds of consumers). In the end, consumers don't care if you're first. Please keep this fact in mind.

Pay attention to these brands and how they are positioned. Some are by attributes. Others are by their personal values. Then there are others who are positioned as the first. Some focus on a specific target market.

Review this section again and study how each is positioned. Take notes and look for examples in your everyday life. They are everywhere. Cool? Cool.

One final note. Remember, this section is about standing out from the crowd. The goal, then, is to determine what will make you stand out and break through the noise.

We will go a little deeper into how you do just that next.

CHAPTER 10

FINDING YOUR POSITION IN THE MARKET

How do you find your piece of consumer real estate? How do you go about finding your position in the market? Well, let's find out.

First, you must realize that every market has competition and the competition is not always another person, company or product. Sometimes you're competing with all the noise in the market. You're in a constant fight to gain the attention of prospective clients, customers, patients, and fans. It is a difficult fight that you can win.

To help you win, I have created a few guidelines that will, well, guide you to your piece of consumer real estate that you can own. Here they are.

(1) YOUR POSITION MUST BE DISTINCT

No one else can claim to be the world's first full time blogger on watches. Ariel Adams, who I mentioned in a previous chapter, owns that spot. Which brings us to an important point. One way to be distinct is by being first in a category.

Coke and Pepsi are insurmountable in the cola category. So, how do you compete in a category where dominant players already exist? You obviously can't be first.

THE CLIMB

Well, you must create a new category and be first in it. Get it?

Well, that's what 7Up did. They became the "uncola". They found a piece of mental real estate and built their brand there.

7UP is distinct in that it is known as the "uncola". Of course, that distinction won't pull many from Coke or Pepsi. But, 7UP isn't trying to do so. They built their real estate in a neighborhood for those who want an uncola. Get it?

(2) YOUR POSITIONING MUST BE BENEFICIAL TO YOUR TARGET

See, being first is great. But you being first must also benefit the customer. Remember, Apple was not first in the MP3 market. In fact, the iPod was literally built with off-the-shelf components. In other words, besides the operating system, Apple didn't have to invent a thing.

So, how does your brand, in terms of positioning, benefit the client/customer?

Fitness coach Jason Robinson is positioned as the guy who knows the shortcuts to a sculpted body. Okay, there are no shortcuts. However, the benefit is that you will look good in a significantly shorter period because you were offered the proper guidance.

(3) YOUR POSITION MUST BE CREDIBLE. BMW can make the claim of making ultimate driving machines. Jason, through his client's figure competition wins has proven he knows the steps to a sculpted body. There are hundreds of people who have succeeded using his system.

Now, this is where your brand story comes into play. Your story tells your audience that you understand their problems and their pain. You have experienced it or you have helped those who have. As such, you are credible.

Here's a key insight: If you can explain the problem better than an investor, client, news anchor, or some other person can, they will instantly see you as credible. So, really understand the problem your audience is facing.

(4) YOUR POSITIONING MUST BE FOCUSED

Specialists tend to do better than generalists, financially speaking. This is especially true in fields like medicine.

Let me break this down. Because you know a lot about a little, you do better financially than those who know a little about a lot. So, focus pays dividends. Are there exceptions? Absolutely. But the rule is clear; specialists do better financially then generalists.

Here are a few ways you can focus:

You can specialize in a certain service offering. Ally Bank doesn't have branches like Bank of America. As such, they claim, at least, that they can save their clients money because of lower fees or no fees in certain banking situations.

Now, in this case, if I were advising Ally Bank, I would have them name this positioning. That way, when people think of online banking, they would think of them. Besides, they aren't the only online bank. Perhaps they can call it "Home free banking" - meaning you don't have to leave your home and you are free of the fees of other banks.

THE CLIMB

You can specialize in a specific industry. As an example, you can create software for architects and engineers.

You can focus on a specific target. David Buer writes a weekly health and fitness blog in the Huffington Post. After his own dream of competing on the U.S. Track and Field Olympic Team was destroyed in a serious auto accident, David developed techniques for helping people with post-injury and post-surgical physical rehabilitation. By the way, notice how his story plays into his focus.

You can focus on organizational size. Small businesses versus big ones and vice versa.

You can focus on a geographical area. A landscaping expert might focus on hot Southern climates.

When you think of electric cars, you didn't think of sporty design. The Toyota Prius, for example, is practical but not sporty. Tesla changed that. They designed a sporty-looking, fast car. Note: Toyota and Tesla are in two completely different target markets. So, the comparison is made to point out design. That's all.

Some insurance companies, like AllState, focus on accident forgiveness.

Some physicians only focus on a specific condition - vein specialists for example.

Remember, the goal is to separate yourself from the competition. You want your target to think of you first when a *specific* problem arises. Right? So, I suggest that you explore all of these possibilities.

NO MAGIC BULLETS

Like all of branding, there is no magic bullet. Your positioning may not fall into your lap or happen over a weekend. It takes time. That being said, how do you do it?

Well, you can position yourself in many ways. We just covered quite a few. But we'll go deeper.

Okay, first, you can position yourself *based upon your personal values* like Dave Ramsey or Lady Gaga.

You can position yourself as the *first* like Ariel.

You can position yourself *based upon some attribute* of yourself. Remember, Volvo focused on safety and BMW the drive. Jason Robinson focuses on sculpting - specifically, exercises that get you there. Another personal trainer may position himself as the *guru of healthy weight gain*. Maintaining a certain weight is important for some sports like American football and rugby where large men are the norm. Also, many bodybuilders put on muscle to compete.

You can position yourself based upon *some target audience*. A person who coaches women record producers would easily gain traction. There are some who help those 40 and over start their first business.

Yes, this is a lot to absorb. That's why you must go back over the examples I've given. To help you even more, we will review a few examples of positioning.

CHAPTER 11

EXAMPLES OF POSITIONING

One of the best ways to understand and solidify your positioning is by studying examples. We will review the process with examples we make up and those that already exist in the market.

Let's start with an example we created. For this example, you're a fitness expert. Of course, you could be an attorney, musician, executive coach, or executive chef. It doesn't matter. The process is the same.

We will start the positioning process by looking to your values and your story.

Let's say that restoration is a core value. Your story is about how you helped a loved one bounce back from a catastrophic injury. If restoration is a core value of yours and you have cared for a person who is bouncing back from a catastrophic injury, this might be a great place to start.

For example, you may position yourself as the personal trainer who helps *restore* people back to health after a catastrophic injury or health event like cancer.

See how those two came together?

THE CLIMB

Now, they may not always fit so nicely. That's why it's important that you look at various ways of positioning your brand.

BE THE ONLY ONE

Okay, when positioning yourself, you always want to answer this question: Am I the only one? In other words, "am I the only one who does this?" Being the only one automatically positions you. When you're the only one, you don't have to worry about being the best, whatever that means.

Here's an example: Am I the only one who helps restore people back to fitness after a heart attack, cancer fight or car injury? You can also combine this positioning with a geographic attribute. You might be the only one in Atlanta or Orlando.

Let me tell you how powerful that positioning is. Once you send out a press release as being the only one, every news organization will beat your door down for a story. It's not the typical unbranded stuff. You have an angle - an angle that's easy to grasp and difficult to duplicate.

As I stated earlier, there are many ways to position yourself or stand out. You might, for example, be the only yoga instructor who works with professional athletes. In other words, you help them with relaxation and flexibility. We can go on and on.

See how useful and practical this stuff is?

But, there's much more. In the next chapter, we will discuss another element of branding: personality.

STEP 4: BRAND PERSONALITY

CHAPTER 12

BRAND PERSONALITY INTRODUCTION

Product, or non-human brands, are a lot like people. They have personalities. Some are cool, like Apple and others are intelligent, like IBM. Remember, IBM engineers are the people behind the supercomputer, Watson.

GEICO, using its little gecko, is comedic. So is Progressive Insurance with Flo and other characters.

Mutual of Omaha is conservative.

Take cigarettes. Marlboro is masculine while the Virginia Slims brand is feminine.

Axe body spray is about seduction.

Of course, people have personalities. Some are adventurous, like billionaire businessman Richard Branson, and others are loud and in your face like fitness expert Jillian Michaels.

Podcaster Pat Flynn is kind and soft spoken. He never uses profanity. Gary Vaynerchuck is the complete opposite. He is full of energy, is blunt, and uses profanity, a lot. They both are successful.

THE CLIMB

The point is, personalities are a critical part of branding. For one, they help tie, more strongly, the personal brand to the target. It puts forth your authentic self which breeds credibility and trust - two critical aspects of powerful personal brands.

In addition, your brand personality is a differentiating factor. When you book Seth Godin, who is cerebral, you get a different personality than when you book Gary Vee, who is street smart.

Your brand personality also helps shape expectations. For example, you expect Dwayne "The Rock" Johnson to be a tough, funny guy in movies. That's the personal brand he has developed over the years.

When you go to a Donnie and Marie show, you expect wholesome, family-friendly entertainment. There will not be sexually suggested lyrics or questionable dancing to concern yourself with.

You expect Clint Eastwood to be rugged. This is a role he has played his entire career. Ruggedness, by the way, is his personality on and off the screen.

And, we expect Sofia Vergara to be both sexy and comedic. Some may substitute the word sexy with glamorous. I won't argue the difference. The point is, comedy is at the center.

PERSONALITY TYPES: WHICH IS YOURS?

Here's a list of different personality types. Of course, this list is not exhaustive, but is a guide.

Adventurous
Richard Branson

Protector
Johnson & Johnson
Samuel L. Jackson

Masculine
Dwayne "The Rock" Johnson

Wholesome
The brother/sister team of Donny & Marie Osmond

Comedic
Kevin Hart
Kevin James
Will Farrell
Mike Epps

Rugged
Clint Eastwood

Sexy
Sofia Vegara

Cool
Denzel Washington

Again, this list is illustrative, not exhaustive.

Okay, we have some important work ahead: discovering your brand personality.

CHAPTER 13

DISCOVERING YOUR BRAND PERSONALITY

The best way to determine your brand personality is to allow others to help you. That's because we are not particularly good at self-assessment. We think that we are, but, we're not. We simply can't see ourselves as we actually appear.

Even if you are good at assessing yourself, you still need confirmation. Remember, the key here is authenticity. Why risk it.

A WORD, OR TWO, ABOUT YOUR BRAND PERSONALITY
Here's the process: First, note that this exercise is designed to help unearth obvious personality types. See, if you're going to infuse your personality into your brand, it must be authentic. If your personality type is not obvious after this exercise, then I would caution you on experimentation.

The point of this exercise is to add to your brand, not subtract from it. The only debate should be on subtle differences. For example, some may call Sofia Vergara glamorous instead of sexy. That's fine. Still the comedic part of her personality is obvious in her television ads and her interviews.

So, if after this exercise you don't know your personality type, I would continue as you already have. Again, experimentation is

THE CLIMB

dangerous. You are who you are. Either your personality will reveal itself pretty easily or it won't.

DISCOVERING YOUR BRAND PERSONALITY

Okay, here's the process: Ask at least three friends or colleagues to imagine walking into a high school cafeteria.

There are groups of kids at various tables. Each table is dominated by a specific personality type.

So, you have the cool, wholesome, masculine, comedic, rugged, sexy, glamorous, nurturing, serious, nerdy, conservative, and athletic kids sitting at their own table.

Ask your friends and family which table would you belong?

Again, your personality should be obvious. As I stated before, one can argue over whether you are a nerd or intelligent personality type. And yes, they will manifest themselves differently. But that's not the same as being a nerd type to some friends and a jock to others. That's where you must be really careful.

What you're looking for is consistency. If three friends land on the same personality type, that's a pretty good sign of where you are. Can you be both a nerd and comedic? Yes. Definitely. However, you only want to brand one type unless a dual personality type is your brand.

For example, there are comedians who are nerds and they are funny. So, that is a perfect example of both. However, most people will present strongly with one.

SAY HELLO TO MY PERSONALITY

Now, introduce your personality. Begin by infusing your personality into your tweets and FaceBook posts. Remember, this is the test phase. Pay attention to the engagement you get.

Here are a few examples of brand personalities:

Chef Carla Hall is always smiling, and her tweets are fun and happy. On the television show The Chew, now cancelled, she was the one who was most likely to dance. Again, that's her personality.

Gary Vaynerchuck is loud and intense. His videos and Instagram posts and stories all show him as he is. If Vaynerchuck was to suddenly stop using profanity, he would lose 80% of his audience.

Photographer Chase Jarvis is an adventurous-creative. He is always chasing the new in fun and interesting places. He became famous by shooting photos of active sports for Toyota and other big brands. Again, clients know what to expect from him. His personality is always on display.

Next is Dr. Oz. I wanted to first remind you about his personal values. Specifically, authentic health information. Now, in terms of his personality, Oz is approachable. He is quick to hug or place himself in silly situations. And that's why so many celebrities are willing to open up to a cardiovascular surgeon.

As you go through your day, pay attention to how personal brands display their personality. The better brands always do. After all, it is their personality that attracts a lot of people to them.

THE CLIMB

Now, how will prospective fans, clients, customers, and patients identify you in the future? Well, that's what identity is all about. We will learn about this important branding element next.

STEP 5: BRAND IDENTITY

CHAPTER 14

BRAND IDENTITY

Award winning actor, musician, and comedian Jamie Foxx is currently the host of a television show called Beat Shazam. The purpose of the game is to identify a song before the app Shazam can. For those who aren't familiar with Shazam, I'll explain.

Shazam, which is an app that first appeared on the iPhone, is a song recognition app. What it does is pure technology genius. Let's say you're riding in your car or sitting at home and a song comes on. You've heard it before but don't know the title or the artist. No problem. Simply fire up Shazaam, press the listen button, and, in most cases, it will tell you the title and artist. Incredible.

Well, the show is the same. Except in this case, contestants, three couples, compete for a million-dollar prize.

Again, the goal is simple: identify the song before Shazaam can. Sounds easy? It's not. That's because you're only given three seconds, at best, to identify the song.

What's important about Shazam and the show, for our purpose, is identification. The show proves that we can recognize complex input quickly.

See, being able to identify our parents, friends, and, yes, foes, is, from an evolutionary standpoint, a matter of survival. When we

THE CLIMB

see something that we recognize, a person, product, or symbol, it makes us feel safe.

The opposite is also true. We instinctively stay away from those things we don't recognize or, again, that we know presents a form of danger. This phenomenon is especially true for brands.

In order to attach to certain brands, be it personal or product, we need a way to identify them at some point in the future. We need to be able to say, "Yeah, that's Coke. I already know what it's going to taste like. I'm safe buying it."

Speaking of Coca-Cola, if you were to do a blindfold test, you could still easily identify an old Coca-Cola bottle. The bottle's curvy shape is so distinctive that it's unmistakable upon touch. This shape is a part of Coke's identity. It helps us to identify it in the future.

When Apple introduced its iPhone X, many people complained about the black notch that sits at top. However, no matter where you are in the world, that notch instantly tells you that's it's an iPhone X and not some other phone. Of course, as usual, others will soon copy Apple. In fact, some have already introduced variations of the notch in their own phones.

The shape of a bottle is just one way brands use to help consumers identify their offerings. They also use names, logos, symbols, fonts, colors, packaging, signatures, structures, door handles, signs, and sounds, just to name a few, to identify their products and services. They also use business cards, letterhead and websites. These identity pieces alert us to the fact that we have the right product. We're safe. We can consume it.

As you might have guessed, personal brands also have identity pieces. Perhaps the most well-known is that of the Jordan brand logo. But Jordan is not alone. Tiger Woods, wedding gown designer Vera Wang, Oprah, and fashion designer Tori Burch, just to name a few, also have distinctive styles, logos and symbols.

Well, as a personal brand, you need identity pieces as well. They are what we will discuss next.

CHAPTER 15

THE BRAND IDENTITY PROCESS

All personal brands or brands in the making need identity pieces. Yes, that includes you. Your audience needs a way to distinguish you from others on sight. So, let's go.

To get started with your brand identity pieces, grab your brand elements. If you haven't gone through the process of developing them, no matter how crude, do so now. The rest of the process won't be effective until you have.

Here are the brand elements you need to have in order to continue:

- Values
- Story
- Positioning
- Personality

A FEW KEY QUESTIONS

A quick note before we begin. Every question that you answer from this point on is for you to eventually give to a graphic designer in the form of your brand identity guidelines. Why? It's simple: most personal brands do not have graphic design experience. Even if they do, they are not particularly good at producing the best work for themselves.

Yes, hiring a graphic designer is going to cost money. But it's not as expensive as you might think. There are resources like 99 designs and Fiverr ($5 per gig) where you can procure great graphic design at a good price. Besides, if you're serious about building a personal brand, then this cost is nominal and absolutely essential. Also, a professional can save you a tremendous amount of time - time you can spend bringing in revenue.

So, in the end, you are going to provide a graphic designer, through your answers to questions I'm going to ask, with your identity guidelines. These written guidelines will provide the designer with a clear picture of the direction of your brand.

In the end, you will hand or send the graphic designer your written guidelines for what you want in your identity pieces. Now, you may only want a logo. Still, I highly recommend that you write and provide guidelines. That's because as you grow, so will your needs. You won't have to stop and do all the exercises again. You can simply point to your guidelines. Nice, right?

Cool. Let's do this.

To begin, I want you to answer a few questions. Again, the answers to these questions will become your guidelines. Got it?

1. WHO IS YOUR IDEAL CUSTOMER?
Think of an ideal customer, client, fan or patient. What do they look like, in terms of gender, fashion, etc.

What do they like to do for work or play?

What do they watch on television?

Brand Identity Process

Which magazines, if any, do they read, whether printed or digital?

Do they read books? What type? Fiction or nonfiction? A specific genre?

What about social media? Where do they hang out? What type of posts causes them to engage? Are they bystanders or active participants? Which platform?

Remember, for each question, you are attempting to make life easier for the graphic designer and you. You are painting a picture of who your identity pieces are most likely to be in front of. Got it?

Let's continue.

2. WHAT IS THE BIGGEST PROBLEM, FRUSTRATION, STRESS, PAIN POINT, OR OBSTACLE FACING YOUR TARGET AUDIENCE?

How and where do they express this frustration? How can you express your understanding of this problem graphically? A series of memes? Specific photos? Instagram stories? Tweets? LinkedIn posts?

An example is people expressing their hair problems on Twitter. Some will even post pictures. That's a clear sign that they are seeking help.

Twitter, by the way, is a great place to unearth your target's problems or pain points. Just do a search on what you believe the problem or pain might be. If you don't know, ask them. Or, better yet, observe. They will eventually complain about a product they're

THE CLIMB

using or a service that sucks. Pay attention to these moments of venting. They are branding gold.

3. WHAT FIVE VALUES BEST DESCRIBE YOUR BRAND?

Your values affect the colors and overall look and feel of your identity pieces.

Early on, Apple competed with IBM and their Microsoft operating system. As more PC vendors came into the market, their computers performed the same as their competitors. After all, in the personal computer market, there were essentially two operating systems at play: Apple and Microsoft.

The PC market was somewhat an open system and the dominant player. So, naturally, budding entrepreneurs built their companies using Microsoft's operating system and components from the same sources as their competition. Remember the red apples? Same thing.

To make matters worse, these computers, using Microsoft DOS and later Windows, were complicated and certainly not designed for the casual user.

Apple changed the market with one campaign: Think Different. They were different because, for one, their machines were graphically oriented and easy to use. Ease of use became a branding attribute for Apple.

This core value, thinking differently, catapulted Apple to unprecedented success. When everyone else was slapping new stickers on the same red apples, Apple created products that were truly different. And the market responded.

4. WHAT DO YOU WANT PEOPLE TO THINK WHEN THEY INTERACT WITH YOUR BRAND?

Do you want them to think speed, safety, relaxation, or order? What specifically do you want them to think? Give this some thought.

By the way, this is where your positioning comes heavily into play. Revisit how you want to be positioned in the market. For example, Calvin Klein is positioned as the brand for the young, beautiful and fit. They are famous for shirtless male models with great bodies and feature beautiful women.

Speaking of women, when they leave a Beyonce or India.Arie concert, they leave inspired. When men watch Tom Brady or Steph Curry perform, they see the value of hard work. How they are positioned influences our thinking.

5. WHAT DO YOU WANT THEM TO FEEL?

Remember, people don't buy products or services, they buy outcomes. Outcomes are about how they feel about something. How or what do you want them to feel? Do you want them to feel healthier, smarter, richer, thinner, stronger, faster? Again, what specifically, do you want them to feel? List it.

Colors are great for expressing a feeling or outcome. Healthy Choice, for example, uses green to denote health. Robert Kiyosaki uses the colors purple and yellow in all his products. When you see those colors on a book or course, you think of Rich Dad Poor Dad, the mega-selling book series.

Birds Eye Steam Fresh uses blue as the backdrop but is accented with green. The store Fresh and Easy uses green as well.

THE CLIMB

By the way, have you ever noticed that fast food restaurants play in the same color scheme? Yeah, look around on your next car ride. Red, yellow, and white, right? That's definitely not by accident.

6. FROM A PERSONALITY STANDPOINT, HOW ARE YOU PERCEIVED?

What type profile pic would best express your brand personality? Photographer Chase Jarvis is cool and laid back. His profile pics reflect his personality.

Lynda.com looks, well, like the founder, Lynda. Lynda wears glasses and is reading a book in the logo. She embraces the nerd personality and it has served her well.

Oh, by the way, she and her husband sold lynda.com to LinkedIn for $1.4 billion. Yes, that's a billion plus. Sweet.

7. IS THERE A CERTAIN GRAPHICAL STYLE THAT SUITS YOUR BRAND?

Author Jorge Cruise always has his hands in his pockets on his book covers. He wears a t-shirt and jeans in all of them. By the way, he has positioned himself as the belly fat cure guy.

Jeff Gitomer is the author of several bestselling books on sales. His books have a unique style. First, they are small and have a denim or cloth feel. That had to be expensive to produce. Anyway, another unique feature of his books is the title. Many begin with the words "The Little…." For example, "The Little Red Book of Selling" and "The Little Black Book of Questions" are two of his book titles.

Gitomer differentiates himself through his book styling and his books have a cartoon feel inside.

Author John Maxwell uses the same font and two-color scheme across all his books.

8. HOW CAN I USE PACKAGING TO DEMONSTRATE MY BRAND QUALITIES?

A photographer can deliver her photos in branded packaging. Of course, doing so would be expensive. However, if you're shooting, say, high end weddings the cost is nominal and will separate you from everyone else. That's for sure.

A less expensive option is to have stickers produced by a company like 48-Hour Prints. For a role of 1,000 stickers, it will only cost you around $25 US or so. Then you can place the stickers on plain packaging or envelopes. See how easy that is?

9. BRAND COLORS

Colors communicate powerfully. Some colors immediately evoke smiles and others, tears. A blue box from a certain store will certainly bring a smile while a pink ribbon might remind someone of a friend she lost to breast cancer. Colors matter, big time.

Here is a short list of various colors and their meaning. Take a moment and review them.

Blue
So, IBM made its name in computers, although they're more of a service company now. But when you have computers, security is key. Police and other security organizations use blue.

Red

THE CLIMB

Red represents passion, among other things. Coke reminds us of the power of red.

Black
There are black tie events, limousines and the American Express Black Card which is reserved for those with a high net worth.

Pink
Mary Kay cosmetics uses pink. They even award their top salespeople with pink luxury cars.

10. SHOULD I HAVE A SIGNATURE OR SYMBOL LOGO DESIGNED OR SIMPLY USE MY NAME?

If you use your name, it must be consistent on all media. The font, spacing, and feel must be consistent.

A few notes about personal logos. Make sure that your designer understands your core values, story, positioning and brand personality. Using playful colors and a whimsical font won't be smart if you are positioned as an expert on less invasive heart procedures.

Your logo should capture the essence of your brand. Michael Hyatt's logo, for example, resembles a compass. He literally is about helping you find direction in your life.

My suggestion is that you begin collecting ideas that you will later share with your designer. Pinterest is a perfect location for storing your ideas. In fact, you can create boards and share them with the designer.

For those who don't know what Pinterest is, go to Pinterest.com and check it out. It is a must for most personal brands.

Next, we're going to discuss several action steps you need to take to build a powerful personal brand.

STEP 6: BRAND YOU

CHAPTER 16

ACTION STEPS

Simply going through the steps is not enough to build a powerful personal brand. You must offer your clients, customers, prospects, fans or patients something to watch, read, or hear.

What will they watch, read or listen to?

Well, the secret sauce of powerful personal brands is depositing. They deposit, a lot. That means they offer high value content on a regular basis. In other words, they constantly teach their audience how to get a six pack, handle an out of control teenager, make inexpensive meals and improve one's running technique.

It's this teaching that truly separates powerful personal brands from those that are not. Study any well-known brand and you will discover this pattern.

YouTube sensation Mike Chang has over 500 YouTube fitness videos.

Pat Flynn has hundreds of free podcast episodes.

Dr. Oz provides free, detailed health information on his television show and website.

THE CLIMB

Suze Orman teaches us how to live a better financial life through her books and television programs.

I can go on and on.

TIME TO TAKE ACTION

In this final chapter, I'm going to offer you a few reminders and some action steps to take.

Here are a few reminders:

1. Review your personal values daily and place them into action. Keep a journal of your activities.

2. Blog, post on FaceBook and other social media regularly. I suggest daily. Of course, it's your call.

3. Be consistent among all your social media accounts. Be as consistent as possible with your profile pic, bio, logo, or avatar across all your accounts.

4. Remember, if you are the only physician in town who specializes in veins, say so. Positioning. Remember that?

5. Make sure that your profile pics and bio reflect your brand personality. If you are a fun-loving person, then by all means show it. Review the brand personality section again for ideas.

6. Spend about 30 minutes a week reviewing your competition and surveying the market. Doing so will help ensure that your positioning is solid.

7. Place your identity on all your touch points. A touch point is any way that you connect with your target. So, your business cards, website, blog, post cards, billboards, YouTube videos, match boxes, and t-shirts are just some of the ways you come into contact with your audience. If you touch your target with your message, then place your identity on it.

A FEW ACTION STEPS

1. **Create an introductory YouTube video.** This can be a low production video that you will share on all your social media.

2. **Change your about page.** Here's why? When new visitors come to your blog or website, they're going to check your about page at some point. They want to know who you are. Therefore, your about page must capture their attention.

You see, most about pages are simply chronological accounts of someone's background. They have their work experience, degrees and certifications and a few bragging points in a crude effort to impress. Oh, and they are all written in the third person. Have you ever noticed that?

Well, that stuff is boring. Just think, how many about pages do you remember? The problem is it doesn't serve the needs of the target audience. It doesn't tell a story of how they are connected to you and why you are the right person to help solve their problems.

Go back to the brand story section, step 2, and review the brand stories again.

3. **Become a quoted source.** This is a critical step. Being a media source immediately skyrockets your credibility and spreads your name.

Here's how to do it. Perform a search on terms related to your work. Go to the related articles and blog posts.

Make a list of the reporters and bloggers who show up at least three times. Or, if an article on, say, Inc. magazine appears, contact that writer. Magazines like Inc. and Entrepreneur have a huge audience.

Next, send them an email and share your story, why you are qualified to comment, and a quick brand promise statement - what you promise to deliver. Be clear about how you will help their readers, viewers or listeners.

Reporters and bloggers are always searching for interesting angles on stories and content. Now, if you are an expert in increasing speed by improving running techniques, then mainstream media will be interested in your work when, say, the NFL combine is coming up. They will be looking to fill stories about their hometown teams. This is your opportunity.

Do the same for podcasts and other audio programs.

4. Offer testimonials. Use your brand story to tell how this person helped you. Your name and story will appear in front of thousands and perhaps millions of people, for free. And big-name folk like Tony Robbins will gladly include you. They love testimonials.

A FINAL, FINAL NOTE
There are lots of action steps packed into these pages. My goal was to create a book that will lead to real results. That's why this book is so action-oriented. Sure, I could have given you a lifetime worth of theory. But you are in the real world facing real problems.

Action Steps

In the words of a great 21st century philosopher, "Ain't nobody got time for that."

Now, it's time to act. It's time to read and complete all the action steps I suggest. Some you will grasp right away. Others will take some time. But, don't quit. Take action and you will climb to the top of your market. When you get there, say hello.

It's been a pleasure. Take care.

ABOUT THE AUTHOR

Dwayne K. Sutton is the author of five books and the international bestselling course, The Climb: 6 Steps to a Powerful Personal Brand. He is a brand consultant and business advisor to some of the world's most successful entrepreneurs, business professionals and personal brands. A graduate of Duke University's Fuqua School of Business and a former Ernst & Young management consultant, Sutton is recognized internationally as a thought leader on persuasive communication, business storytelling, and branding. He speaks regularly to colleges and universities, not-for-profit organizations, and major corporations. Sutton lives in Huntersville, North Carolina, a suburb of Charlotte, with his wife and daughter.

CONTACT THE AUTHOR
Email: dwayne@dksutton.com
Facebook: @dksutton
Instagram: @dksutton
Twitter: @dksutton
LinkedIn: linkedin.com/in/dksutton

Made in the USA
Columbia, SC
11 May 2021